AF539848

# SELF-EFFICACY
## THE *CAREER DETERMINER OF STUDENTS*

# SELF-EFFICACY
## *THE CAREER DETERMINER OF STUDENTS*

***By***

**Dr. Akthar Parveen**
*Teaching Associate*
*Deptt. of Education*
*Rayalaseema University*
*Kurnool - 518 002*

**&**

**Dr. Dayakara Reddy**
*Head & Professor*
*Deptt. of Education*
*Sri Venkateshwara University*
*Tirupati - 517 502*
*Andhra Pradesh*

**DISCOVERY PUBLISHING HOUSE PVT. LTD.**
**NEW DELHI-110 002**

***Published by:***
**Tilak Wasan**
**DISCOVERY PUBLISHING HOUSE PVT. LTD.**
4831/24, Ansari Road, Prahlad Street
Darya Ganj, New Delhi-110002 (India)
Phone: +91-11-23279245, 43764432
Fax: +91-11-23253475
E-mail: parul.wasan@gmail.com
info@discoverypublishinggroup.com
web: www.discoverypublishinggroup.com

***First Edition:*** **2011**
**ISBN: 978-81-8356-721-3**

**Self-Efficacy:** ***The Career Determiner of Students***


***Printed at:***
***Shree Balaji Art Press***
***Delhi***

## ***Dedication***

*This book is dedicated to the readers whose constant feed back, suggestions, encouragement, and inspirations augment my morale.*

# Foreword

In modern world industrialisation, urbanisation, modernisation has bestowed man with stressful life. Stress is prevalent in every walk of life. Even the students are not exception to it.

Intermediate stage is a crucial stage where students are prone to immense stress and tension due to overburdened curriculum, and heavy competition.

This study "self efficacy in relation to intelligence, personality and occupational choice among intermediate students" throws light on various factors related to intermediate stage such as self efficacy, intelligence, personality, and occupational choice.

This study is significant as it deals with current problems, career options of intermediate students, who are at crossroads and at transitional stage. The students are inexperienced, though not lacking knowledge but need to be wiser in making a right occupational choice.

The objective of the study is apt, clear and comprehendible. Variables are well conceived. To scrutinize, different variables statistical techniques were used such as

Means, standared deviations, t-values,F-values and multiple regressions.

The findings of the study, and suggestions given were commendable and needs implication. Thesis is thought provoking and laudable.

Finally this book is of immense use to the teachers,

lecturers, students, and academicians of all faculties as a reference book. It enables everybody to know the facts related to occupational choice and develop awareness related to it.

**Dr. DAYAKARA REDDY**
Head and Professor
*Department of Education*
*Sri Venkateshwara University*
*Tirupati-517502*
*Andhra Pradesh*

# Preface

It was rightly said by Stanly Hall that "Adolescence is the period of stress and strain and storm and strife". Intermediate, is a crucial stage in the life of the individual, as the parent's expectations, teacher's academic pressure, student's aspirations, societal needs and heavy competition generate stress among present students.

In modern era stress in educational field is rampant. Many recommendations were put forth by various committees to lessen the burden on the part of the students, because internal stress, work anxiety, overburdencd curriculum unhealthy competition develops mental illness and leading to suicidal tendencies among intermediate students.

A study on "self-efficacy in relation to intelligence, personality and occupational choice among intermediate students" is current topic of research which develops insight into the problem, raising innumerable questions in the mind of academicians, parents, teachers and students. It enlightens the causes of failures, indecisiveness, lack of knowledge related to occupations among various communities with its consequences.

The present book is aimed to identify the influence of certain factors like intelligence, personality, and occupational choice on self efficacy of intermediate students. Data was collected from 1200 senior and junior intermediate students hailing from various colleges.

The subject matter of the book has been divided into six chapters.

In first chapter an effort was made to define various variables involved in study such as self-efficacy, intelligence, personality, and occupational choice and their inter relationship was discussed.

Second chapter presents research reviews in relation to four variables.

Third chapter presents significance of the problem, objectives of the study, hypothesis.

Fourth chapter presents design of the study, data collection procedure, sample used, tools scoring method used and statistical techniques.

Fifth chapter presents results and discussions .related to various hypotheses

Sixth chapter presents educational implications and suggestions for further study.

Any suggestions and criticism will be gratefully welcomed and acknowledge.

**Dr. Akthar Parveen**
*Teaching Associate*
*Department of Education*
*Rayalaseema university-Kurnool-518002*

# Acknowledgements

I deem it great pleasure to acknowledge my profound respect, deepest admiration and sincere thanks to my research supervisor Prof. V. Dayakara Reddy Sir under whose able guidance and supervision my Ph. D. work was completed. His constant encouragement, inspiration guidance helped me to work systematically. I am obliged and indebted to him.

I am thankful to Mr. Samiulla Sir Professor of Department of Psychology-Tirupathi, for his tireless systematic guidance, valuable suggestions, enlightening discussions and innovative ideas which have been instrumental in the successful execution of work.

I am grateful to my beloved husband Mr. Mirza Yusuf Baig for his love, affection, support and co-operation.

I owe my gratitude to my parents for their inspiration and moral support.

I thank my daughters, Mirza Arshiah Yusuf and Mirza Ambreena parveen who are my source of energy, spirit, strength .Without them nothing is possible.

Above all I thank Almighty who is omnipotent and graceful.

**Dr. Akhtar Parveen**

# Content

# INTRODUCTION

"First say to yourself what you would be, and then do what you have to do"- Epictetus Discourses.

When an individual joins the school, one has no choice. When a child comes out of the cocoon of the school, he had to face grim reality of the world outside. There are courses of action to be considered, options to be made, careers to be planned. One has to forget old fairy tales and stero-typed 'bolly-wood' fantasies, and coolly and objectively survey the lay of the land ahead of him.

In planning ones life, it is necessary to neither avoid over-confidence or exaggerated ideas of ones competence as much as diffidence nor underestimate ones ability.

The great Hanuman could not realise the power till others reminded about them. Lord Hanuman did not venture to leap across the sea to Lanka till many admirers pointed out that he was the child of the god of the winds. Correct self-appraisal and self-confidence hold the key to any planning in life. Life is not a gamble; if the best has eluded the second best should be tried. One has to remember the song "Hey, sirrah, sirrah whatever will be, will be."

Success is not possible in life without hard work and sustained effort nothing can ever be achieved without determination, application; honesty and a sense of realism. But realism should not be confused with cynicism or an inferiority complex. Life is not a bed of roses. But it is also not all thorns and snares. It is a challenge. One should not waste time in mere self pity or morbid complaints about others.

Parents are the right persons who guide their children. If they fail to do so then educational and vocational counsellors are available to resolve the differences and guide in the right direction.

## Career Determinents

A Career determines people's lifestyle and the work environment, routine, earnings, job style, comfort, challenges, physical exertion etc.

When an individual is making an occupational choice he is deciding a way of life, a lifestyle. One must be clear about the expectations from the job- power, money, status, discipline, command, or challenge. Unflagging involvement comes with interest and reinforcements come in the form of promotion, monetary incentives, Recognition and involvement. Progress comes with determination as well as concerted effort. Success leads to what is generally termed as 'job-satisfaction'. In choosing a career it is important to know about self and what you want from your profession.

## Changing Trends in Career Choice

The world of work is in a state of flux. Specialisation within each profession has taken over from the general list. Gone are the days when grandfather's profession was handed down through generations, and the family torch had to be carried forward. It is an age of self-identity and self-expression.

## Making Choice-occupational Selection

Every one aspires to choose the right kind of profession. There is crying need in every human being to use their talents and give expression to his personality. Yet many young people stumble or just drift into a job giving little thought to the consequences. They make career decisions for superficial reasons and land up with inappropriate career choices resulting in dissatisfaction and unhappiness. People make poor work choices because they take up jobs without taking themselves into consideration. i.e., Without assessing their aptitudes, interests, and personality. They take-up courses and careers for only some superfluous reasons, e.g. under their friends influence, or to suit their parent's desires or to take the easiest available opportunity.

When reasons are not at all related to self-knowledge and personal needs, choices tend to be distorted. The ultimate consequence of a poor choice in careers results in dissatisfaction and frustration. Dissatisfaction leads to unhappiness, boredom, stress and physiological threats.

Work is a major source of personal identity. While making work choices, one should select those kinds of work where the combinations of aptitude, interest, and personality are strong assets. However, work choices also depend on the opportunity, the urgent needs of the individual at that time. Nevertheless, even in such situation, the individual should not allow themself to 'give up'. He should wait, watch, and be alert, for opportunities to make purposive change and adaptations. This is the 'secret' of all those who rose from the bottom to the top.

Awareness of one's 'true' motivations, aspirations, dreams, strengths, aptitudes, interests, likes, dislikes, limitations and weakness are essential. This awareness must be as specific as possible. It must back by actual evidences, i.e., by actual achievements and behaviour and, if required, supplemented by objective test-results and professional assessments. If an individual accepts a job through a conscious process of assessment, one is less likely to be disappointed and disillusioned later. Choosing the right career or making right occupational choice needs correct occupational information.

## Occupational Information—Aims, Nature

It is the accurate and usable information about jobs and occupations. It refers to facts concerning the importance of vocations, entrance requirements, opportunities for promotion, health and accident hazards, compensation, and other working conditions that are usually met in specific vocation or related groups of vocations.

Aims of occupational information:

- To help pupils to secure meaningful educational experiences through understanding their role in the world of work.
- To help pupils to mature in vocational understanding
- To help pupil to make a suitable vocational selection, preparation, placement, and adjustment.

Occupational information should be given concerning the following items.

- Nature of occupation – its duties and responsibilities.
- Importance of occupation
- Special mental and other abilities required for the job
- Special educational achievements and training required for the job
- Method of entering into the occupation.
- Restrictions for joining the profession-medical fitness, educational qualifications, age, sex, nationality etc.
- Service conditions.
- Special concessions given
- General trend of the employment.
- Average income – starting salary, upper ceiling, and increments.
- Chances of promotion and advancement.
- Pension and other facilities.
- Relation with social progress.

Occupational information is essential because students make the following mistakes in choosing a career.

## Common Mistakes in Occupational Choice

- Selecting an occupation that requires mental ability above than that of the student.

- Choosing an occupation that has limited employment potential.
- Choosing an occupation for which the student does not possess essential skills.
- Choosing an occupation for which the required level of skill cannot be achieved.
- Choosing an occupation for which the individual does not have an appropriate characteristic of personality.
- Choosing an occupation without the required physical strength and endurance.
- Choosing an occupation because of its glamour.
- Choosing an occupation without giving due attention to its financial aspects.
- Choosing an occupation which is already over-flooded.
- Choosing an occupation on the basis of parent's wishes and ambitions.

Hence there is an urgent need for guidance and occupational information services.

Need and importance of occupational information services:

- To make wise and effective vocational choice
- To comprehend rapidly changing social and economic structure.
- For educational planning.
- To plan community programmes

Making right occupational choice is not an easy task. A number of factors effect occupational choice of an individual. Like mental ability, skills, level of attainment, personality traits, physical strength, self confidence, self-efficacy, intelligence and ability, economic status etc.

## Self-efficacy Beliefs and Bandura's Social Cognitive Theory

According to Bandura's (1986) social cognitive theory, individuals possess a self system that enables them to exercise a measure of control over their thoughts, feelings, motivations and actions. This self system provides reference mechanism and a set of sub-functions for perceiving, regulating, and evaluating behaviour, which results from the interplay between the system and environmental sources of influence. As such, it serves a self-regulatory function by providing individuals with the capability to influence their own cognitive processes and actions thus alter their environment.

How people interpret the results of their own performance attainments informs and alters their environments and their self-beliefs which, in turn, inform and alter subsequent performances. This is the foundation of Bandura's conception of reciprocal determinism, the view that Personal factors in the form of cognition, affect and biological event Behaviour and Environmental influences create interaction that results in a triadic reciprocity.

In general he provided a view of human behaviour in which the beliefs that people have about themselves are key elements in the exercise of control and personal agency and in which individuals are viewed both as products and as producers of their own environments and of their social systems Bandura (1986) says,

- People evaluate their experiences and thought process through self-reflection.
- The belief the people hold about their capabilities powerfully influence the way in which they behave
- People can't accomplish task beyond their capabilities simply by their belief.
- For competent functioning individual needs harmony between self-beliefs, proper skills and knowledge.
- Hence self-perception of capabilities and self-efficacy beliefs help to stand first and acquire success in life.

## Self-Efficacy Component of Social Cognitive Theory

The self-beliefs that individuals use to exercise a measure of control over their environments include self-efficacy beliefs-

"beliefs in one's capabilities to organise and execute the course of action required to manage prospective situations" (Bandura, 1997)

Because self-efficacy beliefs are concerned with individuals perceived capabilities to produce results and to attain designated types of performance, they differ from related conceptions of personal competence that form the core construct of other theories. To better understand the nature of self-efficacy beliefs it may be useful to explain how they are acquired, how they influence motivational and self-regulatory process, and how they differ from similar or related conceptions of self-beliefs.

## Sources of Self-efficacy Beliefs

(*a*) **Mastery experience** Bandura emphasized that one's mastery experiences are the most influential source of self-efficacy information and has important implications for the self-enhancement model of the academic achievement, which contends that, to increase student's achievement in school, educational efforts should focus on altering students' beliefs of their self-worth or competence. This usually accomplished through programs that emphasize enhancing self-beliefs through verbal persuasion.

(*b*) **Vicarious experience** it is the effect produced by the actions of others. This source of information is weaker than the interpreted results of mastery experiences, but when people are uncertain about their own abilities or have limited prior experience, they become more sensitive to it. A significant model in ones life can help instill self-beliefs that will influence the course and direction that life will take. Part of one's vicarious experience also involves the social comparisons made with other individuals. These comparisons along with peer modelling can be powerful influence on developing self-perceptions of competence (Schunk, 1983).

(*c*) **Verbal persuasions** individuals also create and develop self-efficacy beliefs as a result of the verbal persuasions they receive from others. Effective persuasions should not be confused with knee-jerk praise or empty inspirational homilies (Bandura, 1997).

This is consistent with Erikson's (1959, 1980) caution that a weak ego is not strengthened by being persistently bolstered and that "children cannot be fooled by empty praise and condescending encouragement". Rather, "a strong ego, secured in its identity by a strong society, does not need, and in fact is immune to any attempt at artificial inflation". Persuaders must cultivate people's beliefs in their capabilities while at the same time ensuring that the envisioned success is attainable. And, just as positive persuasions may work to encourage and empower, negative persuasions can work to defeat and weaken self-beliefs. In fact, it is usually easier to weaken self-efficacy beliefs through negative appraisals than to strengthen such beliefs through positive encouragements (Bandura, 1986).

**(*d*) Physiological states**- such as anxiety, stress, arousal, fatigue, and mood states also provide information about efficacy beliefs. Because individuals have the capability to alter their own thinking, and self-efficacy beliefs Bandura says,

- People live with psychic environment that are primarily of their own making.
- People read themselves and their reading comes to be a realisation of the thought and emotional states that individuals have themselves created.
- Often people gauge their confidence by the emotional state they experience as they contemplate an action.
- When they experience aversive thought and fears about their capabilities it lowers perception of their abilities.
- Ultimately he concludes that the process of selection, integration, interpretation, and recollection of information influence judgment of self-efficacy.

## Efficacy-activated Processes

Much research has been conducted on the four major psychological processes through which self-efficacy effect human functioning.

### (*a*) Cognitive Process

The effect of self-efficacy beliefs on cognitive processes takes a variety of forms. Much human behaviour, being purposive is regulated by forethought embodying valued goals. Personal goal setting is influenced by self-appraisals of capabilities. The stronger the perceived self-efficacy, the higher goal challenges people set for themselves and the firmer is their commitment to them.

Most courses of action are initially organised in thought, people's belief in their efficacy shapes the types of anticipatory scenario they construct and rehearse. Those who have a high sense of efficacy, visualise success scenarios that provide positive guides and supports for performance. Those who doubt their efficacy visualise failure scenario and dwell on many things that can go wrong. It is difficult to achieve much while fighting self-doubt. A major function of thought is to enable people to predict events and to develop ways to control those that affect their lives. Such skills require effective cognitive processing of information that contains many ambiguities and uncertainties. In learning predictive and regulative rules people must draw on their knowledge to construct options, to weight and integrate predictive factors, to test and revise their judgments against the immediate and distal results of their actions, and to remember which factors they had tested and how well they had worked.

### (*b*) Motivational Processes

Self-beliefs of efficacy play a key role in the self-regulation of motivation. Most human motivation is cognitively generated. People motivate themselves and guide their actions anticipatorily by the exercise of forethought. They form beliefs about what they can do, they anticipate likely outcomes of prospective actions. They set goals for themselves and plan course of action designated to realise valued futures.

The three cognitive motivators include casual attributions, outcome expectancies, and cognized goals. People who regard themselves as highly efficacious attribute their failures to insufficient effort, those who regard themselves as inefficacious attribute their failure to low ability. Motivation based on goals or Personal standards are governed by three types of self influences. They include self-satisfying and self-dissatisfying reactions to one's performance, perceived self-efficacy for goal attainment and re adjustment of personal goals based on one's progress.

### (c) Affective Processes

People's beliefs in their coping capabilities affect how much stress and depression they experience in difficult situations, as well as their level of motivation. Perceived self-efficacy to exercise control over stressors plays a central role in anxiety arousal. People who believe they can exercise control over threats do not conjure up disturbing thought patterns. But those who believe they cannot manage threats experience high anxiety arousal. They dwell on their coping deficiencies. They view many aspects of their environment as fought with danger. They magnify the severity of possible threats and worry about things that rarely happed. Through such inefficacious thinking they distress themselves and impair their level of functioning. Perceived coping self-efficacy regulates avoidance behaviour as well as anxiety arousal. The stronger the sense of self-efficacy the bolder people are, in taking on taxing threatening activities.

A low sense of efficacy to exercise control produces depression as well as anxiety. It does so in several different ways. One route to depression is through unfulfilled aspiration. Much human depression is cognitively generated by dejecting ruminative thought. A low sense of efficacy to exercise control over ruminative thought also contribute to the occurrence, duration and recurrence of depressive episodes.

### (*d*) Selection Processes

People are partly the product of their environment. Therefore, beliefs of personal efficacy can shape the course of life taken by influencing the types of activities and environments people choose. People avoid activities and situations they believe exceed their coping capabilities. But they readily undertake challenging activities and select situations they judge them selves capable of handling.

Career choice and development is but one example of the power of self-efficacy beliefs to affect the course of life paths through choice related process. The higher the level of peoples perceived self-efficacy the wider the range of career options they seriously consider, the greater their interest in them, and the better they prepare themselves educationally for the occupational pursuits they choose and the greater is their success.

Occupations structure a good part of people's lives and provide them with a major source of personal growth.

## Effects of Self-efficacy Beliefs

- It influences motivational and self-regulatory process in several ways.
- They influence the choices people make and the courses of action they pursue.
- Beliefs of personal competence also help determine how much effort people will expend on an activity, how long they will persevere when confronting obstacles, and how resilient they will prove in the face of adverse situations. The higher the sense of efficacy, the greater the effort, persistence, and resilience.
- Efficacy beliefs also influence the amount of stress and anxiety individuals experience as they engage in a task and the level of accomplishment they realise.

- Strong self-efficacy beliefs enhance human accomplishment and personal well-being in many ways.
- People with a strong sense of personal competence in a domain approach difficult tasks in that domain as challenges to be mastered rather than as dangers to be avoided, have greater intrinsic interest in activities, set challenging goals and maintain a strong commitment to them, heighten their efforts in the face of failure, more easily recover their confidence after failures or setbacks, and attribute failure to insufficient effort or deficient knowledge and skills which they believe they are capable of acquiring.
- High self-efficacy helps create feelings of serenity in approaching difficult tasks and activities. Conversely, people with low self-efficacy may believe that things are tougher than they really are, a belief that fosters stress, depression, and a narrow vision of how best to solve a problem. As a result of these influences, self-efficacy beliefs are strong determents and predictors of the level of accomplishments that individuals finally attain .Bandura (1986, 1997) has made the strong claim that beliefs of personal efficacy constitute the key factor of human agency.
- Social reformers strongly believe that they can mobilise the collective effort needed to bring social change.
- Innovative achievements also require sense of efficacy. Innovations require heavy investments of effort over a long period with uncertain results.

## Self-efficacy and Career Choice

Self-efficacy beliefs influence the choice of adults and career decisions of college students. Undergraduates choose careers in areas in which they feel most competent and avoid those in which they believe themselves less competent or less able to compete.

### (*a*) Problem-Based Learning

Connecting learning to its application in the workplace is the goal of problem-based learning (PBL) activities. PBL engages the student in investigating a problem situation for which there is not right or wrong answer. The situation raises concepts and principles relevant to the subject matter that reflect real-life issues of the student's world. PBL requires observation, investigation, solution building, and resolution by students who "own the problem" and who must formulate their own solutions. The ill structured problem offers students Opportunities to test their skills and confront the internal and external barriers they may perceive as limiting their successful achievement of a goal or objective.

The instructor's role in PBL is that of a coach and facilitator. As such, the instructor may model a bahaviour, demonstrates a procedure, role play a situation to help students understand a concept, but gradually reduces assistance and transfers the learning responsibility to the student. Observation responses, performance reviews, and other feed back should be given in a way that offers encouragement to the student.

Deficiencies should be presented as avenues for improvement and as a natural part of the learning process.

Brophy (1998) suggested the following strategies for helping students improve self-efficacy beliefs.

1. act more as resource person than a judge
2. Focus more on learning process than on outcomes.
3. React to error as natural and useful parts of the learning process rather than as evidence of failure.
4. Stress effort over ability and personal standards, over normative standards when giving feedback.
5. Stimulate achievement efforts through primarily intrinsic rather than extrinsic motivational strategies.

### (*b*) Community Based Learning

Community based learning experiences are also forms of contextual learning. Examples include project based work place learning, apprenticeships, and social directed worksite learning. Community based learning experiences connect school work to career goals by involving students in solving the real-world problems of the business community.

Kellick and Leibowitz (1998) present six criteria that characterise worksite learning.

1. Learning goals are established through the agreement of the students, teachers and community partners.
2. Projects focus on real-world problems that are of relevance to students and community, and require efforts and persistence over time.
3. Students receive coaching and advice from teachers, employers and community partners, they use the tools and follow practices of experts in the field.
4. Students develop an awareness of the educational requirements of an occupation and of career opportunities in the occupational area.
5. Learning involves the interdisciplinary process of inquiry, investigation, hypothesizing, articulation, collaboration, negotiation, practice and reflection.
6. Achievements are demonstrated through multiple types of assessment.

### (c) Self-monitoring and Self-assessment

Contextual, problem-based, learning practices provide opportunities for students to apply knowledge and skills in the same way they are used in the real world. However, their contribution to self-efficacy is embedded in reflection. Self-assessment, peer reviews, performance checklists, journal writing, and portfolio assessments offer students opportunities to make meaning of what they have learned and enhance their career development. The goal of assessment is empowerment. Portfolios that contain students selected works, for example, allow students to reflect on their performances, compare current with prior work, and recognise their potential for continued growth.

Feedback that is directed to a student progress rather than to a comparison with other classmates work offer guidance for future learning rather than discouragement by emphasizing inadequacies.

## Personality

Talents also have a large hereditary component, and some differences in emotional reactivity may be innate. Parents respond differently to babies with differing characteristics. In this way a reciprocal process starts that may exaggerate some of the personality characteristics present at birth. What happens to the potentialities with which the infant is born depends upon his experiences while growing up. Although all experiences are individual there are two types of experiences.

### (*a*) Common Experience

All families in a given culture share certain common beliefs, customs and values. While growing up, the child learns to behave in ways expected by the culture. One of these expectations has to do with sex roles. Most cultures expect different behaviours from males than from females. Sex roles may vary from culture to culture, but it is considered "natural" in any culture for boys and girls have to be predictable Differences in personality merely because they belong to one or the other sex.

Some roles, such as occupations, are of our own choosing. But such roles are also patterned by the culture. Different behaviours are expected from doctors, truck drivers, and artists. That is to some extent. People feel comfortable in an occupation if they behave as others do in that occupation

### (*b*) Unique Experiences

Each person reacts in his own way to social pressure. Personal differences in behaviour may result from biological differences-differences in physical strength, sensitivity, and endurance. They may result from the rewards and punishments imposed by the parents and the type of behaviour modelled by them. Even though he may not resemble them, a child shows the influence of his parents.

Personality is a very complex psychological concept, difficult to define. It is a concept by which we understand and view ourselves. Normally, external appearance and behaviour are the main characteristics which are used to describe personality. Personality varies and can be seen along a continuum from one extreme to the other in its several dimensions. Personality is the sum total of characteristics that differentiates people or the stability in a person's behaviour across different situations. Personality is the entire mental organisation of a human being at any stage of his development. It embraces every phase of human character, intellect, temperament, skill, morality, and every attitude that has built the course of one's life.

In terms of occupations, people vary in personality types. In terms of sheer tolerance. Some can work endlessly; others cannot sustain themselves through hard work. Matching occupational requirements with personality characteristics is a very important part of career guidance.

## Guidance Needs

"Guidance is a process of helping individuals to understand themselves and their world".

It is life long continuous process which aims to help individuals to understand their personal characteristics, strengths and weakness of their personality and the social environment with which they interact. The main function of guidance as a helping profession lies in the preparation of youth to meet their problems satisfactorily in the present and future. Guidance also helps individual to develop his unique personality characteristics to promote adjustment and develop decision-making competency.

### (*a*) Vocational Guidance

Is a process of assisting the individual to choose an occupation, prepare for it, enter upon, and progress in it. It is concerned primarily with helping individuals make decisions and choices involved in planning a future and building a career-decisions and choices necessary in effecting satisfactory vocational adjustment. It is essential as there are differences among individuals and differences among occupations open to them.

## Personality Factors Effecting Occupational Choice

A number of personality factors effect occupatione of the individual. They are

1. intellectual ability
2. aptitudes or special abilities
3. influence of schooling
4. child rearing practices
5. self-concept
6. values in work
7. stereotypes and expectations
8. interests
9. realism
10. sex differences
11. environment influences
12. socio-economic status

Theories of career development are of great value as they develop insight into the reasons students are motivated to make certain career choices.

Anne roe's theory, emphasis on childhood determents of future vocational choice. The family environment and the training given to the child in early years sets the pattern of personality which will play a decisive role in the choice of future career. Rejection, acceptance, dominating and democratic attitudes of parents towards their children lay foundation for certain personality characteristics and these characteristics are important for certain types of occupation.

## Personality Type and Occupational Choice

Holland classified six personality types and matched them with occupations.

### (*a*) The mechanical personality type

Individual is aggressive and likes physical activity. Requires skill, strength, and coordination. Such people prefer engineering, technical and mechanical jobs.

### (*b*) The investigative personality type

Prefers activities which require thinking, organising, and understanding rather than feeling or emotion. Such personality types are scientists, in their outlook and can go in for careers which are oriented to research leading from higher studies.

### (*c*) The social personality types

They like interpersonal interaction rather than intellectual or physical activities. Service professions are best suited for this personality type. They may also consider international affairs, Foreign Service, journalism.

### (*d*) The conventional personality type

They enjoys activities which are rule regulated, e.g., finance, accounting, banking, actuarial, etc.

### (*e*) The enterprising personality type

They influences others and wants to have power and status. Administrative services, law, public relations, business management and politics are professions which would be ideally suited.

### (*f*) The artistic personality

They are involved is self-expression, artistic creation or emotional activities. Artistic professions are those related to the arts, drawing, painting, music, drama, writing, etc.

Tiedemann and O'Hara's theory said "career development is a process of fashioning a vocational identity through differentiation and integration of the personality as one confronts the problem of work in living".

## Intelligence (Mental Ability)

The performance of the students in a class is usually judged by their achievement score in the examinations, which is often considered as their academic achievement. This is considered as main basis for admission and promotion of a student to his/her next class. It has also been taken as a criterion even in selection of the individuals into various vocational and professional courses.

Intelligence is the ability and capacity to learn and carry out abstract thinking to respond appropriately to a new situation.

There are many factors which influence the career choice among which intelligence is one of the most important factors. Every profession needs a certain level of intellectual abilities without which an individual cannot function efficiently. For selection of the subjects, for selections of courses, in vocational selection, and career choice intellectual abilities remain a significant factors. It has been reported by guidance personnel that children with high intellectual abilities aspire to high-level occupations and duller children are more interested in lower level occupations. Individual aptitudes, influence of schooling, family influences self-concept, values stereotypes and expectations, interests, realities related to different occupations differences in sex, environmental influences also affect occupational choice.

Right choice at right time makes individual's life happy. Exact self analysis of ones abilities, ones intelligence bestowed through heredity, healthy mental attitudes, and good personality traits, positive self-efficacy beliefs promote individual in their life and shower success in every walks of life.

Keeping in view the prominence of the variables the researcher has selected the topic "self-efficacy in relation intelligence, personality and occupational choice among intermediate students" to investigate the relation and effect of the variables.

# CHAPTER 2 REVIEW OF RELATED LITERATURE

The major goal of formal education is to equip students with the intellectual tools, efficacy beliefs, and intrinsic interests needed to educate themselves in a variety of pursuits throughout their lifetime. It requires high intelligence, good personality traits, positive self efficacy beliefs, and effective occupational choice.

A number of studies were conducted to find out the relation between self-efficacy, intelligence, personality, and occupational choice.

## Research Reviews on Self-efficacy

Bandura (1986), emphasized that ones mastery experiences are the most influential sources of self-efficacy information, which has important implication for the self-enhancement model of academic achievement, which contends that, to increase students achievement in school, educational efforts should focus on altering students beliefs of their self-worth or competence.

Schunk (1981) study on persuasions involve exposure to the verbal judgement that others provide are a weaker source of efficacy information than mastery or vicarious experiences, but persuaders can play an important part in the development of an individual's self-beliefs.

Brown &Inouye (1978) observed that a model's failure has a more negative effect on the self-efficacy of observers when observers judge themselves as having comparable ability to the model. If, on the other hand, observers judge their capability as superior to the model's capability, failure of the model does not have a negative effect.

Zeldin &Pajares, (1997), individuals also develop self-efficacy beliefs as a result of verbal persuasions they receive from others.

Erikson (1959, 1980) caution that a weak ego is not strengthened by being persistently bolstered and that "children cannot be fooled by empty praise and condescending encouragement. Rather a strong ego, secured in its identity by a strong society, does not need and in fact is immune to any attempt at artificial inflation.

Hackett &Betz (1989) assessed self-efficacy beliefs by asking individuals to report the level generality, and strength of their confidence to accomplish a task in school setting.

Shell, colvin, &Brunung (1989) assessed self-efficacy beliefs by asking to perform reading or writing tasks.

Bandura, (1989) assessed self-efficacy beliefs of students in self-regulatory strategies.

Meece, wig field &Eccles, (1990), assessed self-efficacy beliefs by asking students to report how well they expect to do in an academic subject.

Harter, (1982) assessed self-efficacy beliefs by asking whether they understand what they read i.e. perceptions of competence.

Marsh, (1992), assessed self-efficacy beliefs by asking whether they are good in academic subject i.e. academic domain specific self-concept.

Meece, (1990), assessed self-efficacy beliefs by ability perceptions.

Lent & Hackett (1987) rightly observed that specificity and precision can be purchased at the expense of external validity and practical relevance.

Bandura (1997) argued that efficacy beliefs are multifaceted and contextual, but the level of generality of the efficacy items within a given domain of functioning varies depending on the degree of situational resemblance and foresee ability of tasks demands.

Lent et al. (1993) showed how efficacy judgements can be tailored to varying levels of academic outcomes and still remain highly predictive. They compared student's confidence to succeed in math-related course with three career related outcomes intention to take the courses listed on the instrument, Grades obtained in math related course that students took during the subsequent term, and interest in the math course listed on the instrument. Self-efficacy beliefs were predictive on each account.

Reyes, (1984) used the term self-efficacy and self-concept as synonymously.

Harter, (1990), described the concept of self-concept as a generalised form of self-efficacy

Marsh et al. (1991) compared the direct effect of achievement on the math self-concept and self-efficacy of fifth graders and reported a stronger direct effect on self-concept that on self-efficacy.

Chapmen and Tunmer (1995) found that the reading performance of beginning readers during their first year of schooling had a stronger effect on their subsequent self-efficacy than on their reading self-concept.

Relich (1983), cited in March (1990), assessed math self-concept and math achievement, performance on a mathematics task, and self-efficacy for the task. Achievement correlated equally strongly with domain-specific self-efficacy and self-concept. Specific performance on the math task was more strongly correlated with specifically assessed self-efficacy that with domain-specific self-concept

Pajares and Miller (1994) used path analysis and found that item-specific math self.-Efficacy beliefs were more predictive of a mathematics problem-solving than were domain-specific self-concept beliefs.

Mone, Baker, and Jeffries (1995) also reported that self-efficacy had greater predictive validity for academic performance then did self-esteem.

Zimmerman, (1992), Schunk, (1989), (1996), Shunk, and Hanson &Cox, (1987) drew a distinction between self-efficacy for performance and self-efficacy for learning.

Bouffard-bouchard (1990) experimentally induced high or low self-efficacy in college students by providing positive or negative feedback and found that students whose self-efficacy had been raised used more efficient problem-solving strategies on a novel task and outperformed students whose self-efficacy had been lowered.

Skaalvik and Rankin (1996) subjected self-concept items and domain-specific self-efficacy items to confirmatory factor analysis and discovered that they loaded on the same factor, leading them to conjecture that the two may be different measures of the same construct. These findings led them to suggest that the traditional distinction between self-concept and self-efficacy may have been overstated in the literature.

Graham and Weiner (1995) observed, what cannot be disputed is Bandura argument that self-efficacy has been a much more consistent predictor of behaviour and behaviour change than have any of the other closely related expectancy variables.

Collins (1982) identified children of low, middle, and high mathematics ability who had, within each ability level, either high or low mathematics.

Self-efficacy. After instruction the children were given new problems to solve and an opportunity to rework those they missed. Collins reported that ability is related to performance. But that regardless of ability level children with high self-efficacy level completed more problems correctly and reworked more of the ones they missed.

Bouffard-Bouchard, Parent and Larivee (1991), found that students with high self-efficacy engaged in more effective self-regulatory strategies at each level of ability

Berry (1987) revealed that self-efficacy enhances student's memory performance by enhancing persistence.

Lent, Brown &Larkin (1984,1986), in studies college students who pursue science and engineering courses, high self-efficacy has been demonstrated to influence the academic persistence necessary to maintain high academic achievement.

Zimmerman (1991) and his associates have been instrumental in tracing the relationships among self-efficacy perceptions, self-efficacy for self-regulation, academic self-regulatory process, and academic achievement

Rosenberg & Zimmerman,, 1992, Zimmerman 1989, 1990, 1994, Zimmerman &Bandura, 1994, Zimmerman Martinez-Pons, 1990; Zimmerman &Ringle,1981 this line of inquiry has successfully demonstrated that self-regulatory efficacy contributes to academic efficacy. For example, Zimmerman, Bandura, Martinez-Pons (1992) used path analysis to demonstrate that academic self-efficacy mediated the influence of self-efficacy for self-regulated learning on academic achievement. Academic self-efficacy influenced achievement directly (=.21) as well as indirectly by rising student's grade goals (=.36) other researchers found that self-efficacy is related to self-regulated learning variables(feather 1988;Ficham & Cain, 1986, Paris &oak, 1986, Pint rich &Schrauben, 1992, Pokey & Blumenfed;1990 Schunk,1982, 1985).

Finding in this area suggest that students who believe they are capable of performing academic tasks use more cognitive and met cognitive strategies and persist longer than those who do not (Pint rich & Garcia, 1991). Pintrich and Degroot (1990) reported a correlation between academic self-efficacy and both cognitive strategy use and self-regulation through use of Meta cognitive strategies. Academic self-efficacy also correlated with semester and final year grades. In class seat work and home work, exams, and quizzes, and essays, and reports. Pintrich and De Groot concluded that self-efficacy played a "facilitative" role in the process of cognitive engagement that raising self-efficacy beliefs might lead to increased use of cognitive strategies and, thereby higher performance. And that "students need to have both the will and the skill to be successful in classrooms".

Some researchers have assessed judgments of self-efficacy in terms of particularised self-perceptions of competence highly consistent with their criteria task being assessed. This assessment requires that, if the criteria task involves solving specific mathematics problem, the efficacy assessment asks students to provide judgments of confidence to solve similar problems, if the task involves reading comprehension, students are asked to provide judgments of their perceived capability correctly answer various questions that tap comprehension of the main ideas in a Passage (Schunk,& rice 1993; Shell, Murphy, & Burning, 1989) if the task involves writing an essay , students are asked to provide judgments that they possess the various composition, grammar, and mechanical skill on which their writing performance is assessed. (Pajares &Johnson, 1994, 1996, Pajares &valiant, 1997, in press, Shell et at.1989, 1995.)

Schunk (1996) and his colleagues have reported on numerous studies that have examined the role of particularised self-efficacy beliefs in various academic contexts. Schunk (1981) used path analysis to show that modeling treatment increased persistent and accuracy on division problems by rising.

D.A.Adeyemo and Bolaogunyemi (1985) worked on study "emotional intelligence and self-efficacy as predictors of occupational stress among academic staff in a Nigerian university". The study seeks to explain the interactive and relative effects of emotional intelligence and self-efficacy on occupational stress of university academic staff.

The results indicated that the two independent variables, when taken together, were effective in predicting occupational stress. Each of the variables contributed significantly to the prediction of occupational stress with self-efficacy making higher contribution to the prediction of occupational stress. On the basis of this finding, it is suggested that emotional intelligence programming and self-efficacy intervention techniques will benefit teachers immensely in coping stress.

Hong, Traci (1990) in their study on "the influence of internet self-efficacy and search task on locating credible health related information online" explored the effect that internet self efficacy and search task specificity have on the self-efficacy outcome and performance of finding online health related sites which contain attributes of web site accountability as established by the AMA. When search task specificity was taken into account, there was an internet self-efficacy and task specificity interaction where high internet self-efficacy participants locate sites higher in web site.

Accountability in the general search task (the more complex search task) than their low self-efficacy counterparts. There was no significant difference in credibility perceptions for the specific search task (the less complex task). High internet self-efficacy participants demonstrated better online performance than their low internet self-counterparts.

Valley, Hayashi, Garner-Holman, and Giacobbi (1998) studied on "sport confidence" the athletes rated, first, achievement (includes self-mastery and demonstration of ability), second, self-regulation (includes physical/mental preparation and physical presentation), and third, climate (includes, social support, coaches leadership, vicarious experience, environmental comfort and situational favourableness) in order of perceived priority as the most important sources of improving sport confidence.

Nancy E. Betz & Karla L Klein the Ohio university Karen M Taylor (2000) study on decision making self-efficacy scale describes the development and evaluation of a short from of the widely used career decision-making self-efficacy scale (CDMSE Taylor &Betz 1983). the psychometric characteristics and relationship to the career decision scale (CDS Osipow 1987 ) and the vocational identity scale (Holland, Johnston,& Asama, 1993) the potential utility of a more efficient short form of the scale for use in career counselling interventions will be discussed.

Kang, Jeonghee (1998) in his study on memory self-efficacy and memory performance in older males reported secondary analysis of data on 157 males from a larger, study of predictors of memory performance in community-dwelling elders. Measures included depression, memory performance, Meta memory, and memory-self-efficacy. An unusual finding was the multimodal distribution of memory self efficacy strength scores. The high efficacy groups were significantly younger had larger scores on capacity (+ = high capacity and change (+ = greater stability) these findings provide new evidence that the memory self-efficacy of aging males influences their perceptions of cognitive performance related to memory.

Lent Brown & Hackett's (1999) The study of the effect of family environment, personality and self-efficacy on career indecision of college students is designed to investigate the utility of social cognitive theory to the understanding of career decision. The purpose of the study was to test a casual model of environment and person factors that incorporated key elements of social cognitive theory to career indecision of college students.

By means of a structural equation model. Hypothesis regarding specific direct and indirect influences among family Environment constructs. i.e., (Family relationship, family structure,), personality constructs (neuroticism, extraversion, openness, agreeableness, conscientiousness), self-efficacy constructs (technical and scientific self-efficacy, aesthetic self-efficacy), and career indecision chronically indecision, developmental indecision, global indecision) were investigated.

G.V. caprara, (1999) The study on the role of perceived cognitive and environmental barriers on the self-efficacy beliefs as shapes of children's aspirations and career trajectories is a structural model of the network of sociocognitive influences that shape children's career aspirations and trajectories. Familial. Socio-economic status is linked to children's career trajectories only indirectly through its effect on parent's perceived efficacy and academic aspirations. The impact of parental self-efficacy and aspirations on their children's perceived career efficacy and academic aspirations. Children's perceived academic, social, and self-regulatory efficacy influence the types of occupational activities for which they judge themselves to be efficacious both directly and through their impact on academic aspirations. Perceived occupational self-efficacy gives direction to the kinds of career pursuits children seriously consider for their life's work and those they disfavour. Children perceived efficacy rather than their actual academic achievement is the key determinants of their perceived occupational self-efficacy and preferred choice of work life. Analysis of gender difference reveals that perceived occupational self-efficacy predicts traditionality of career choice.

Don E Bradley and James. A. Roberts (1987) worked on self-employment and job satisfaction: investigating the role of self-efficacy, depression, and seniority. They said first self-employed persons should enjoy higher job satisfaction than others. Second, a portion of the association between job satisfaction and self-employment should be explained by higher levels of self-efficacy and by lower levels of depression among the self-employed compared to others. Third, self-employment veterans are a select group and should be different systematically from self-employment new comers with respect to reported job satisfaction. Findings offer support for the first and second arguments above but not the third. Post-hoc analysis suggests that among the newly self-employed, the association between job satisfaction and self-employment depends on both the quantity and quality of time invested in the business. Implications of these findings and directions for further research are needed.

Kristine Haertl (2002) worked on persons with mental illness often experience disruption in daily occupations. Routines and habits. This article presents results of two separate studies designed to explore time use and occupations of person's either mental illness living in Japan and America. Common themes emerged including the importance of engagement in normalising occupations, the role of productive activities in contributing to life satisfaction, the need for structure amidst opportunities for personal occupational choice. And the relationship between a lack of daily routine and personal dissatisfaction. The literature is reviewed and the studies are summarized, compared, and discussed in relation to implications for occupational therapy.

Tricia prodaniuk, Ronald C Plotnikoff, john C Spence, Phillip M Wilson (2006) worked on the influence of self-efficacy and outcome expectations on the relationship between perceived environment and physical activity in the workplace. Recent research contends that ecological approaches may be particularly useful for understanding and promoting physical activity participation in various settings including the workplace.

Yet within the physical activity domain there is a lack of understanding of how ecological environment factors influence behaviour. Thus the purpose of this study was to examine the relationship between perceived environments, social-cognitive variables, and physical activity behaviours.

Florida state university has worked on self-efficacy, vocational interests, and ability self(2007) the study investigated the relationships among self-efficacy, interests and ability self-estimates in career decision making as measured by the self-directed search and strong interest inventory participants were 239 colleges students enrolled in psychology course at a large public university. The RIASEC structure of interests and self-efficacy was found to be similar due to strong positive correlations among the constructs. Ability self-estimate and self-efficacy was also positively correlated. Features of the SII and the SDS in relation to career decision making and career counselling reanalysed and discussed.

Susan D.Phillips and Anne R .Inhofe (2007) worked on women and career development it reviews the vocational experiences of women as they have been revealed in the literature during in the past decade. The review considered primarily empirical literature findings are sampled relative to women's self-concept development, readiness for vocational choices, actual choices made, work-force entry, experiences at work, and retirement.

## Research Reviews on Intelligence

Cohen (1959) made an analysis of the factorial structure of the Wechsler intelligence scale for children (WISC) at ages 7.6, 10.6, and 13.6. Five Correlated factors were found consistently in three age groups verbal comprehension I and II, perceptual organisation, Freedom from distractibility, and a quasispeciofic factor. These were essentially the same factors that were found in adults on the Wechsler adult intelligence scale. A second order general factor (originally British) accounted for about one-third of the total variance. And about a half of the 'true' variance of the WISC. This factor had a loading pattern very similar to its adult counterpart, being measured chiefly by the essentially verbal sub-tests. It was found that children exhibit a substantially smaller degree of generality of intellectual functioning than do adults, a finding that is directly counter to previously established research results.

Kaufman (1975) factor analysed WISC-R at ages 6 and half to 16 and half (n=200 per age group). The factor structure was remarkably consistent across the age range, with three factors emerging for each age group. Verbal comprehension, perceptual organisation and freedom from distractibility. These factors resemble the factors identified for the 1949 WISC, although the WISC-Structure was more stable and in closer agreement with Wechsler's verbal-performance dichotomy than was the structure of its predecessor. The results of the study are discussed in terms of their clinical applications, particularly interpretation of WISC-R profiles.

The results of the WISC-R factor analysis provide support for Wechsler's sub-division of the tests into verbal and performance scales and for his combination for the various verbal and non-verbal tests to obtain a full scale IQ. Support is also offered, in general, for the clinician's practice of interpreting the specificity of a test when evaluating a child's profile of scaled scores. The structure of the WISC-R is at the same time both consistent with, and a decided improvement over the structure of its highly successful predecessor

Hagen and Kaufmen (1975) administered the WISC-R to 80 retarded youngsters ranging in age from 6 to 16 years. Scaled scores on the 12 tests were correlated, and the matrix was subjected to several factor-analytic techniques. The three factors identified for normal children in a previous study of the WISC-R (verbal comprehension, perceptual organisation, and freedom from distractibility) also emerged for the retardates, although some differences were observed in distractibility factor.

The WISC-R factor structure for retardates was also similar to the structure of the 1949 WISC that was identified for several groups of institutionalised and non-institutionalised retardate. The results of the studies involving the 1949 WISC were reviewed critically to help understand the implications of this study.

The major finding of the above study was that the WISC-R factor for the retarded children was similar to the WISC-R factor identified for normal children (Kaufman, 1975) and also to the WISC factors identified for groups of institutionalised, non- institutionalised retardates (Baumeister and Bartlett, 1962). The similarity to the structure of the 12949 WISC for retarded individuals should provide clinicians with a sense of continuity in the interpretation of the WISC-R. The fairly close congruence of the WISC-R factors for different groups suggests that there may be no qualitative differences in the structure of intelligence for the normal and retarded children. Such a finding, which must first be replicated with other retarded samples before being accepted as a fact, has important theoretical implications. It was also of practical significance, since quantitative treatment of WISC-R score comparison of the IQs obtained by normal and retarded groups is contingent upon the assumption of a comparable underlying structure.

Finally, the factor analysis of the data obtained on retarded children and adolescents offered broad support for Wechsler's IQ scale in the WISC-R. The emergence of the verbal comprehension and perceptual organisation factors gave strong evidence for the construct validity of the WISC-R verbal and performance scales. The large unrated first factor in the principal factor analysis, feature loadings of .44 -.74 for the 12 tests supported Wechsler's combination of the separate scales into a single full scale. IQ substantial correlations between the verbal comprehension and perceptual organisation factors in the oblique rotated solutions (0.44 for oblimax and 0.35 for biquartimin) offered further support for the use of an overall IQ for retarded youngsters.

Silverstein (1969) in his first study analysed the standardisation date for the WISC.WAIS and WPPSI, and obtained a two-factor solution that was much more stable than Cohen's (1959) classic five factor solution. In the second study, Silverstein (1973) analysed the WISC and WAIS date of several groups of mentally retarded individuals and obtained both two-and three-factor solutions, again, the solution with fewer factors was more stable.

Silverstein (1977) studied the additional evidence on the relationship between descriptive efficiency and statistical invariance by analysing the standardisation data for the WISC-R the Wechsler intelligence e scale for children revised (Wechsler. 1974). Inter-correlations among the 123 subtests of the WISC-R for 200 children were found in each of 11 age groups, ranging from 6.5 through 16.5 years in the standardisation sample using the principal-factor method. Silverstein applied the same method for analyzing the data as he used in his earlier studies. Both two-and three-factor solutions were obtained for each age group, using the max plane method, and the stability of the two solutions from one age group to another was assessed by calculating coefficient of congruence. The two-factor solution proved somewhat more stable. But the difference was relatively small and some may actually prefer the three factor solution.

Silverstein (1980) also took up study on cluster analysis of the Wechsler intelligence scale for children revised with hope that additional insight into the structure of the WISC-R might be gained by turning from factor analysis to cluster analysis. The inter-correlations among the 12 sub-tests of the WISC-R were analysed for each of the 11 age groups in the standardisation sample. Clusters were found that corresponded to the verbal and performance scales, but there was also some evidence of a third group of sub-tests, drawn from both scales. The results were in general agreement with those of previous research in which factor analysis was applied to the same data.

The results of other investigators factor analysis of the standardisation data are equally divided on this point. Wallbrown, Blaha and engine (1975) presented a hierarchical solution in which two group factors corresponded closely to the verbal and performance scales.

## Research Reviews on the Factors Relating to Intelligence of School Going Children

Minority group children represent the heterogeneous groups of children so that it becomes difficult to know that group or groups of children should be so classified. The label "minority group children" is used to designate individuals whose values, customs, patterns of thought, language or even interests are significantly different from the prevailing pattern of the society in which they live.

The use of such labels as culturally handicapped, culturally disadvantaged, or culturally deprived to designate minority group children has been unfortunate, because these terms have value implications. No one has the right to degrade a subculture that does not conform to the patterns of the minority group.

Although intelligence testing still constitutes one of the important links in the educational chain, some believe it must be discarded because it allegedly has become tool of the white majority – a tool that is being used to suppress the rights of ethnic minority children and in particular, of negro children (Davis, 1971, Williams, 1970a) the issues concerning intelligence testing of minority group children are compels,. For they are woven into the very fabric of society.

Kent and Davis (1957) administered four WISC performance scale sub-tests in the home and intellectual development. The only significant finding was that the children coming from normal homes obtain significantly higher IQs (MIQ=110) than those coming from overanxious homes (MIQ=101). Most children coming from unconcerned homes (8 out of 9) showed signs of emotional disturbance, such as apathy and lack of spontaneity. The less efficient WISC performance of the children from overanxious homes was attributed to their deficiency in practical abilities. Overall, the results indicated that discipline in the home significantly affected intellectual development.

Wender. Pedersen and Waldrop (1967) studied that boys who were socially dependent at age 2 tended as 6 year olds to have a less abstract cognitive style and lower WISC performance scale IQs, but not lower verbal scale IQs, than boys who were less dependent.

Belmont and Marolla (1973), with their large data set, were able to rule out socio-economic status as a significant factor in birth order effects, but they did not suggest factors or processes that might have explained their interesting results. Belmont and Marolla discovered a strong relationship between birth order and intellectual performance. They correlated birth order data and Raven progressive matrices (culture fair intelligence test) scores of over 300,000 Dutch military inductees. They came from families ranging from a single child to 9 children. Belmont and Marolla found in general that the brightest children came from the smallest families, and within a given family size. The brightest children usually were the first born. There was a gradual decrement in which the 1st of a large group usually obtained the lowest scores in order to control possible hereditary and socio-economic influence, the subjects were separated into 3 groups according to their father's occupation, professional and white-collar, manual, and farm workers. While the scores were highest for the professional and white-collar group, followed next by manual group and lowest for the farm-workers, these differences were obliterated when birth order was the independent variable. The first born of all 3 groups had the highest IQ, followed by the second born and so on down, in general.

Mc Call, Appelbaum and Hogarthy (1973), Mehrotra and Maxwell (1949), Thurston and Jenkins (1929) found that gaps between children affect their intellectual level leads to the prediction that IQ scores of twins and of triplets should be generally lower than the population average.

Record et al. (1970) made a study which compared IQs of children born singly with IQs of twins and triplets. The average IQs were 100 for the single born. 95.7 For over 2,000 twins and 91.6 for 35 triplets. One can therefore see that, on the whole, the order of birth seems to be related to intelligence.

Studies in India have focused their attention on caste differences and by large the results obtained by Rath, Singh, Sin ham, Das and others tended to show that the high caste pupils achieved better scholastically, than the low caste and the tribal pupils. The results of their studies also suggest that the low caste and the tribal pupils are intellectually inferior i.e obtain lower scores on intelligence tests.

Shuey (1958) referred to 72 studies in which a total of 36,000 Negro children were tested and the average IQ was determined to be 85, strongly suggesting a genetic difference. Shuey (1966) further reviewed 382 studies and concluded that the Negro children were one standard deviation or 15

IQ points lower to the whites. Even when SES was controlled, a difference of 11 points remained.

Studies of Gordon (1923), Tomlinson (1944), Hebb (1949), Thorndike (1951), Haggard (1954), stelter (1959), Deutsch (1960), Bruner (1961), Kleinberg (1963), Douglas (1964), Das (1973), Das and Singh (1974), sinha and shukl 1974) and sinha (1975) found improvised environment of the disadvantaged people causing inferior intellectual development. Hebb (1949) argues that the inner city child was immersed in an early impoverish3ed environment which was marked by insufficient stimulation, thus producing retardation so that in effect the child's IQ remained relatively low throughout his life.

The work of Douglas (1964) on a sample of 5,000 children born in one week of 1946 proved that environmental handicaps continued to operate cumulatively in mile childhood. They did not merely affect test performance at 8 years but produced still more marked differences at11 years. They correlated with actual increase or decrease in ability between 8 -11 years.

Thorndike (1951) found that ecological correlations tended to be higher for intelligence scores than for scholastic achievement, demonstrating extreme sensitivity of the measures IQ to the total social environment. This research finding was confirmed by Dutch and Brown (1964), Roberts (1948), Robinson and Meenes (1947) and others emphasizing that socio-economic variable correlate highly and positively with IQ ranges in Negro samples. Das and Singh (1974) also found that besides poverty, social disadvantages suffered by the lower caste children have vital detrimental influence on their cognitive competence.

Having Hurst and Moor field (1967) hold that differences in intelligence test scores between the disadvantaged and the non-disadvantaged groups were not due to differences in their capacities, but of experience, motivation, values and learning styles. Poorly educated and economically deprived parents failed to provide their children the necessary stimulation and experiences that were important in school environment. The limited verbal engagement in the home would restrict a significant aspect of mental growth as measured by intelligence tests. When certain non-verbal tests of intelligence were substituted, the lower class children, who were poor scholastically, displayed normal learning abilities.

Davis (1978) selected various intelligence test problems on which the deprived children did poorly and rewarded them in terms of familiar to the deprived children. Even though these changes produced a test was more attuned to them, inner-city children did not improve markedly.

Appelbaum and Tuma (1977) compared the validity of the Peabody with the WISC and WISC-R for two socio-economic groups. In their study, 40 normal 10 years old children (2- male and 20 female, half of whom were from high and half from low socio-economic status) were compared for performance on the Peabody, the WISC and the WISC-R. IQs obtained on form A and B of the Peabody correlate highly and thus the two Peabody forms are essentially parallel and equivalent forms. Large differences in IQ between children from low socio-economic background and those from high socio-economic background were obtained on all four tests. The Peabody IQs were closer in magnitude to the WISC-R IQs than to the WISC in the low socio-economic group. The results support administering the Peabody to children for obtaining valid IQ estimates.

Covin (1977) found the relationship of Peabody and WISC-R IQs of candidates for special education (90 low achievers in southern elementary schools.). Correlations ranged from a low of .06 between Peabody Form B and WISC-R performance IQ to a high of .59 between the Peabody form-A and WISC-R verbal scale IQs.

Covin and hatch (1977) found the IQ differences in full scale WISC for 500 black and 300 white southern children from families of low income and aged 6 through 15 years, who were referred for psychometric assessment, are reported, and three distinct trends observed. The difference between

IQs of these blacks and whites tended to increase from ages 6 through 15 years. The black children tended generally to decrease in IQ from ages 6 through 15, while the white children tended to increase in IQ from ages 6 to 12 and then decrease through age 15.

Covin (1977) compared WISC and WISC-R scores for thirty, 8 and 9 years old institutionalised Caucasian children. This study compared WISC and WISC-R scores of a typical group of 30, third and fourth grade school children. All 30 were Caucasian children who were in a private

Child care institution in south central Alabama. The 15 females and 15 males ranged in age from 98 months to 1210 months, the mean age being 102 months. They were from low socio-economic homes which had been or were being dissolved due to crisis. E.g. desertion by parents. Death of parents chills abuse. No significant differences between the WISC and WISC-R IQs were present. Thus for such children as these, IQs on the WISC can be expected to be about the same as those on the WISC-R.

Nicholson (1977) arrived at significant correlations between the quick test and the WISC-R when forms 1, 2, and 3 of the quick test and the WISC-R were administered to 62 subjects, ages ranging between 72 months and 195 months, mean age 138 months, 52 black and 10 white children. Correlations between all forms of the quick test, the three scales of the ISC-R and the sub-tests were all positive and significant. Correlations ranged from low of 0.394 to a high of 0.790.

Hatch and Covin (1977) compared WISC and Peabody IQs of three groups of young children from differing socio-economic status levels and or intellectual levels. For the total sample of 67, correlations of 0.88, 0.91 were obtained between the Peabody and WISC verbal, performance and full-scale IQs respectively. The Peabody IQs correlated 0.74 with the WISC full scale for the middle-range of intelligence (kindergarten. Those of higher socio-economic status in a child study centre showed the highest correlations 0.57

between Peabody and WISC performance scale IQs. For more deprived children from head start IQs on their Peabody and WISC verbal scale correlated0.63.

Horton and crump (1962) found that SES and educational level of the parents were more highly correlated with IQs of their children than with race. Ornstein (1965) observed that IQs derived from intelligence tests show inferior performance of lower class children. A high proportion of lower class children score in the slow learner or retarded learner category and there is no improvement in their IQs as they move through grades. In the upper grades and high school, the average IQ of low SES group is likely to top with 20 or more points below that of higher statue groups.

Metfessel (1965) explains that lower class children learn generally slow and owing to this they have trouble with intelligence tests that require speed to follow a sequence of instructions. Then, these low SES subjects disregard the importance of completing the test in time. Jensen (1969) found that economic status was related positively to intelligence. He also observed that children from the middle to upper socio-economic classes used reasoning and abstraction much more than from the low socio-economic classes and were quite proficient in associative learning (Jensen, 1971).

Hammond and Cox (1967) confirmed the importance of social class, mental ability and inter-personal competence as factors in educational achievement. Dave et al. (1970) studying intelligence and academic achievement of children from different SES found that these variables were significantly related to SES. Simon and Simon (1975) obtained significant relationship between SES and academic achievement and SES and IQ.

Knife and Stroud (1959) found that when SES was controlled the correlation between intelligence and grades was not lowered and on the other hand, when intelligence was controlled, the correlation between SES and grades was lowered.

After partialling out the influence of intelligence, Chopra (1964) and Mathur and Hundal (1972) found a positive correlation between academic achievement and socio-economic background. Intelligence and socio-economic background were found to determine to a great extent, the obtained achievement scores.

However, the results of Barial's (1966) study showed no social class difference in scholastic achievement when the effect of intelligence was controlled. Chtterji, Mukherji and Benerji (1972) reported that economic condition of the family seemed to have no effect upon the scholastic achievement of the children in VI and VII classes from all three ability groups.

Explaining the relationship between intelligence, achievement and SES, Mc Cleland (1958) suggested that mental ability may be a foundation as a threshold type of variable with respect to academic achievement. There is a certain minimal level of mental ability which may be required to achieve in school. Beyond this point, the obtained correlation between intelligence and achievement may be due to uncontrolled variability of factors such as socio-economic status.

Morris and clarisio (1977) found improvement in IQs of high-risk, disadvantaged preschool children enrolled in a developmental programme. 17 preschool children who had been previously identified as having notable delays or difficulties with development participated in a remedial nursery school programme. Each child spent on an average 9 months in the programme during which he received individualised instruction and treatment for specific problems. Parental involvement was encouraged and enrichment activities were emphasized throughout the course of the programme. Comparison of participant pre-and post programme was done. Stand ford – Binet IQs showed a significant increase on completion of the remediation.

## Research Reviews on Personality and Managerial Effectiveness

Personality reflects the nature of a personal adjustment to the interpersonal and situational demands of an individual's environment. Personality measures seek to estimate a person's typical behaviour pattern in adjusting to the interpersonal or social aspects of his work environment.

Personality has been defined either as the effect the person has on the other people, Or as the total of his habits. Gibbs, 1955 and Vroom 1959 noted that subordinate personality characteristics, particularly authoritarian and need for independence, affected the relationships between participation on the one hand and satisfaction and effectiveness on the other. Subordinates with dependent authoritarian personality preferred production centered supervision to participation.

Cronbach (1960), classified tests according to their purpose as users to determine how well and how much a person can perform. Such tests do have correct and incorrect answers. For example personality tests useful for managers include, intelligence, verbal ability and numerical ability, in order to map taxonomies of human abilities measured by maximum performance tests Nash (1965) is less pessimistic about the usefulness of vocational interest measures to predict managerial effectiveness. He found that more effective managers have patterns of vocational interest distinguishing them from less effective managers.

Nash (1965), Guion and Gattier (1966), have reviewed the results obtained with personality and interest measures in measuring managerial effectiveness, and found that these measures have not proved themselves as predictors of managerial effectiveness.

Jorgensen (1966), listed adjectives to describe the type of person most likely to succeed as key executive in top management. Most descriptive adjectives of successful executives are decisive, aggressive, self-starting, productive, well informed, determined, energetic, creative, intelligent, responsible, clear thinking, least descriptive adjectives of successful executives are cheerful, formal courteous, modest, amenable, conforming, neat, reserved, agreeable, conservative and kind minded.

Giselle (1966) classified tests into a few broad categories, and jobs into similar broad groupings based on gross estimate of relative similarity in jobs demand. Tests were classified according to 1. Intelligence, 2, spatial and mechanical aptitudes.3, perceptual accuracy, 4.motor abilities and 5. personality and interest. The summary of all studies of execute effectiveness is that measures of intelligence and of personality and interests may be "good bets" as potential predictors of managerial effectiveness.

Moss (1972) found that managerial success was related to initiative, communication skills, decisiveness, motivation and persistence.

Batlies (1979) examined the differences in personality attributes between supervisors who placed equal emphasis on the people and task dimensions of leadership and those who tend to be exclusively people or task oriented with leadership behaviour. Descriptive questionnaire and 16-personality factor, measures on supervisors found that a preference for a balanced style tend to be more in tough minded, practical, conservative and group dependent than unbalanced leadership style.

Chakravarthi et. al (1984), assessed personality variables related to the management role. To find a single personality profile for all managerial positions or different profiles for different categories considering the diverse activities performed by managers of various designations on three different groups, viz., formal, technical and finance background found that differences between the three groups were insignificant, and a single profile could be used as descriptive norms for the model personality patterns. This personality profile depicts management personnel as attentive, insightful, and intellectually adaptable.

Emotionally mature, stable, and unfrustrated at average levels of anxiety.

Paul (1981) investigating the effect of personality on managerial effectiveness by using Giselle's personality inventory. they are supervisory ability, initiative, self-assurance and decisiveness and found that these four dimensions of personality are significantly related to managerial effectiveness.

It is not possible for any manager to do all things, to all men. Each executive has a unique patterning of abilities, skills, attitudes, habits, etc.one manager gives his men a comfortable feeling when things are predictable and highly structured, whereas, that of another put his men at ease, when things are informal and free wheeling. One likes to be closely associated with subordinates and others maintain distance.

Rymarz, (1985) investigated the possibility of relationship between personality traits and levels of execution of professional tasks. Subjects were divided into two groups, effective and ineffective and California personality inventory (CPI) was administered to measure aspects of personality determining level of functioning. Delta questionnaire was administered to measure generalised expectations concerning locus of control. Depending on their degree of expression, personality traits were found to exert a positive or negative influence on professional effectiveness. Comparative analysis of test result revealed essential differences in the personality of structure of the two groups of subjects.

Smith et.al. (1985), found that the use of 16-personality factor-form A, has general objective to the use of personality characteristics for personal selection.

Mohan et al, (1985) analysed managerial effectiveness in relation to occupational goal values of public and private educational institutions and found that intrinsic goal values did not determine managerial effectiveness.

Prakash et.al, (1986), investigated the nature of the relationship between personal values of employees and organisational outcome in banking organisation and found that personal values such as personal enhancement, conformity and dharma had a low to moderate relationship with personal and organisational outcomes.

A manager's job effectiveness is determined not only by his personal attitude but also characteristics of his job, his situation and by his organisations motivational policies and practices. Managers are intended to success at work and personality appears to be an ingredient in such success. In order to understand person-job-personality fit, individuals at first are to be assured that organisations have model personalities.

Inderrieden et al.(1987), studied personality characteristics of work group managers and work group dimensions and found that personality characteristics of the managers were almost strongly related to work group characteristics assessing work responsibility.

Derr et al. (1987), discussed several of managerial styles, acknowledge the motives of underlying worker behaviour and improving the match between the persons and jobs. Four basic personalities are described as 1.gettingahead, 2.getting secured, 3.getting free, and 4.and getting balanced. It is recommended that managers diagnose career orientation by examining an employee's motives, talents, values, and personality constraints and with that employee try to achieve the optimum career orientation.

Beehar et al. (1987), explored the effects of managerial styles. keeping all variables common on two organizations and found that rank and file employees perceptions and attitude behaviours were more favourable in the organisation with the more democratic formal managerial styles than in the more traditional organisations, but there was a little difference in the response of the superiors between the two environments.

Sass kin, Marshall (1987), discussed 1.what makes a leader successful in terms of revitalising an organisation and creating a place where employees want to contribute their best and to whether there is difference between effective leader and managers and revealed that it is an appropriate combination of individual personality, behavioural skills and situational factors that best describes the successful leaders.

Mathur (1987) examined the relationship between managerial effectiveness and leadership styles and self-actualisation among Indian middle level managers of public sector and found that leadership effectiveness was not significantly related to self-actualisation. It was suggested that lack of self-actualisation was due to lack of self-control, over the environment and non-fulfillment of lower level need (physiological security and social esteem).

Using Giselle's personality inventory (SDI) for middle level managers Bowin et al. (1987) found that all the traits in the inventory are useful to measure personality characteristics of successful managers.

Bush et al. (1988) studied the personality profiles of marketing vs. research and development managers. They found that there were some similarities and significant differences between the two groups. Marketing managers were more effective, assertive, venturesome, spontaneous, happy go lucky, enthusiastic, self-opinionated and dominating than research and development managers. These differences could potentially, seriously impair the ability of managers from different areas of productivity interest with each other.

Singh and Satvir (1989) identified some variables affecting managerial success. The criteria for managerial success were number of promotions, career progress and length of service. The investigators found that successful managers tend to be intelligent, reserved, placid, radical, relaxed, power oriented, younger and better educated. The seven factors associated with managerial success are: 1.emotional stability, 2.intrinsic values, 3. anxiety, 4.introverts-extroverts. 5. Intellectual efficacy, 6.power vs. achievement and 7. Conservatism vs. radicalism.

Gable et al. (1990) studied managerial achievement on Machiavellianism and internality – externality on store managers and found that there was no significant correlation between locus of control and managerial achievement. There was a significant correlation between locus of control and Machiavellianism for men but not for women. Men proposed a higher internal control orientation than women.

Yergoror et al. (1990) defined personality traits that were conductive to successful performance and psychological capability with their shipmates and three traits were identified: 1.business, 2.communicative, and 3.reflexive qualities. The specific characteristics of personality traits reflecting professional and the appraisal of motivation was analysed and found that the appraisal of performance and professional motivation should take into account the specific character of competence and socio-psychological adaptability.

If managers are to be effective, they rank the roles they engage in within the contingencies of the situation. It must be recognized that the manager himself is an important variable to consider his approach to managerial effectiveness. An effective manager is one who is aware of the kinds of behaviour and actions which lead to organisational results and who then choose to engage in those appropriate to the environment, the particular managerial job, situation and his own personal preferences (mintzburg, 1973, Campbell et al., 1970).

Radha Krishna, (1992) found that the personality characteristics of high, moderate and low managerial effectiveness groups (N=110) did not differ significantly on intelligence, cyclothymiacs , ego strength, surgency, super ego strength, but the sex and the age showed a significant difference on managerial effectiveness.

Okechuku (1994), studied the relationship of six managerial characteristics to the assessment of managerial effectiveness in Canada, Honkong, and China, and compared the influence of western conceptualized managerial abilities, traits and motivations to assess effectiveness. Managerial characteristics studied include supervisory ability, achievement motivation, intellectual ability, self-actualisation, self-assurance and decisiveness. Several factors were significant predictors of managerial effectiveness in both Eastern cultures and Canada. Senior managers in China were quite similar to their counterparts in Canada but differed from those in Honkong in their use of these characteristics to infer the effectiveness of their subordinates. The most important predictor of managerial effectiveness ratings was self-actualisation in Canada, self assurance In Honkong.

## Personality Traits of Teachers

Charters and Waples (1966) studied the personality traits of teachers. They evolved a link of 15 personality traits of teachers for classroom effectiveness. They are buoyancy, considerateness, co-operativeness, dependency, emotional stability. Ethicalness, expressiveness, flexibility, forcefulness, judgment, mental alertness, objectivity, personal magnetism, physical energy, drive and scholarship.

Borg (1957) conducted a study on personality and interest measures related to criteria of instructor effectiveness. He found a correlation of >71 between the rating of teachers and that of supervisors.

Ryan's (1960) research exemplified the transition from research paradigms that focused almost exclusively on teacher personality traits t0 those that directed inquiry towards the investigation of both teacher attitude and behaviour.

The Mandsley personality inventory was given to first year University students over 3 years by Savage (1962) and the scores on this were related to academic performance at the end of their first year. The results showed that Australian University population had higher mean neuroticism and extroversion scores than the norms of the tests. Analysis of variance and correlation techniques showed that high scores on both factors were negatively related with academic performance.

Getzel's and Jackson's (1963) broad findings consistently revealed that good teachers possess positive personality characteristics and interpersonal skills. the influence of teacher's classroom personalities on children's behaviour, particularly at the primary and elementary school levels was studied by Anderson and Brewer (1965). In order to obtain objective measurement of teacher's classroom personalities and concomitant children behaviour, 26 teacher behaviour categories and 29 children behaviour categories were developed by which both teacher and pupil verbal and non-verbal behaviours might be categorised.

Anderson (1965) divided teacher behaviour into 2 main kinds, integrative and dominative .Integrative behaviour of the teacher expanded the children's opportunities for self-directions and for co-operative behaviour with the teacher and their peer dominative behaviour tended to restrict children's activities and to lead to distracted aggressive , non-cooperative.

Levine (1971) analysed the intelligence, personality characteristics and motivation of pre-service and in-service teachers and compared them with persons working in the other fields. These two differ according to the sex, level of teaching area of speciality and perhaps more significant of, institutional affiliation.

Wayne and Blankenship (1972) in their study made a comparison between ideological orientation and personality characteristics of teacher acception and rejection of B.S.C.S. Biology. B.S.C.S biology programme possesses favourable attitude towards the content philosophy and teaching methods advocated in the programme. Teacher attending institutes were defined as acceptors and teachers who had unfavourable attitude programme were called 'Rejectors'. They measured tolerance capacity for status, social presence achievement via independence intellectual efficiency, flexibility etc., by using the instruments California Psychological inventory (CPI) by Gough and Pupil Control Ideology Form (PCI). They found that acceptors were more humanistic.

Barbara, Sherman, Robert and Blackburn (1975) analysed the personal characteristics and teacher effectiveness of college faculty. Students in a co-educational liberal art college rated faculty on two typical teaching instruments and on a semantic differential form. Data were come from 1500 student judgments on 108 men and women faculty and found that there was significant relationship between Personal Characteristics and teacher effectiveness of college faculty.

Clapp (1977) listed out 10 qualities as the components of good teaching personality namely-dress, personal appearance, optimism, reservedness, enthusiasm, fairness of mind, sincerity, sympathy, vitality ands scholarship.

Robinson and Michael (1987) investigated the personality traits of American secondary teachers and administrators who work in the association of American schools of South America (AASSA). Subjects were divided into 3 group's viz. 17 newly recruited teachers. 71 teachers already working in AASSA schools and 22 AASSA superintendents and principals. The 16PF questionnaire and personal data form were administered. The investigation showed that newly recruited males and females differed from U.S. norms on nine and seven factors. Secondary teachers who apply for overseas teaching jobs were already different from U.S. norms.

Guyton, John William (1988) made a study on "comparison of the personality traits of secondary school teachers in Mississippi public schools" the main purpose of the study was to identify the personality differences between outstanding science teachers. Regulated certified science teachers and provisional certified teachers of science. They found no significant difference existed in the personality traits of the 3 groups as measured by each important factor of Cattle's 16PF questionnaire. The outstanding teachers group was more abstract in thinking self-reliant, independent, resourceful, preferred thinking their own decisions. Proper, moralistic. Aggressive and preferred hard-working people. Discriminate analysis was used to identify six personality factors that combined and differentiated the outstanding and regular groups on the factors B, Q2, O, H, G and I.

## A Few Personality Studies of Teachers in India

Some researches have been conducted in India during the last few years on teacher's personality. In this study an attempt has been made to review some of the studies on the personality of teachers.

Saxena (1969) made an attempt to study the attitudes and personality of teachers. He used Cattell's contact personality factor (form 'A' Hindi version) a coefficient of correlation of +.60 with factor 'H' and +.42 and +.36 with factors 'A' and 'H' respectively were obtained. With high teaching competence. These correlations were +.60 and +.36 respectively. Which show a curvilinear relationship It shows that a very high scores on factor 'H' is typical of less component teachers and only a moderately high 'H' is characteristic of a more successful teacher.

Kaul (1972) made a factorial study of certain personality variables of popular teachers in secondary schools,. His objective was to differentiate the personality traits of popular and unpopular teachers. He used Cattell's 16PF questionnaire. He came to the conclusion that the effectiveness of popular teachers was with respect to attitude toward teaching. Public examination results of their students and the appraisal of their work as teachers respectively.

Tripathi (1972) administered the 16-PF test (form-A) to 52 teachers-trainees and 52 experienced teachers to compare the personality profile of working teachers and teacher trainees. The technique of profile matching was employed for smooth comparisons between the two groups. Only eight factors (A, E, F, G, I, L, and Q4) out of 16 personality factors distinguished the experienced teachers easily. These teachers were conscientious, persistent, sensitive, effeminate, suspecting, jealous, sophisticated, and polished. The experienced teachers were significantly lower from the general population on factor-A, E, F, and Q4 and were aloof, stiff, submissive, soft hearted, glum and serious respectively.

Chhaya (1974) compared effective and ineffective teachers with respect to personality adjustment, teaching attitude and emotional stability. Eight effective and 100 ineffective teachers were selected from 20 randomly selected schools of Kanpur district. Effectiveness and ineffectiveness were known on the basis of high school examination results (board of examinations of 1968, 1969, and 1970) she came to the conclusion that effective teachers had significantly better personality adjustment and favourable attitudes towards teaching. They were less interested in teaching than ineffective teachers, emotionally stable. More authoritarian and extrovert. She found that sex and age of a teacher were significantly related to her effectiveness.

Goyal (1974) studied some of the personality correlated of creativity in secondary school teachers under training. He was interested in knowing specially the personality differences in relation to sex and subject group as well as creativity differences in relation to sex and subject groups. He applied Cattelles' 16-PF questionnaire and Torrance tests of creative thinking as the tools. His sample consisted of 500 student teachers (200 male and 300female) in the age range of 10 years to 47 years. He found that the personality differences between high and low creative persons did not enter teacher training colleges. Intelligence was found to be the most consistent personality correlate of creativity. Highly flexible student-teacher was more guilt prone and less imaginative. Highly creative females were having more self-conflict. Were moralistic, socially precise and bold. Higher intelligence, emotional stability and tough mindedness were common personality traits found in science and mathematics groups at higher and lower levels of creativity.

Srivastava (1974) used 16-PF questionnaire for 52 pupil teachers and 52c experienced teachers to know the impact of professional experience on the modification of personality traits. He found that experienced teachers differed on factors A, E, F, H, Q1, Q2, from the pupil teachers.

Singh (1974) made a comparative study of the personality profiles of married and unmarried high school female teachers. He derived the personality profiles of these teachers with the help of Cattelle's 16-PF questionnaire. The investigator found that the unmarried female teachers differed significantly on factors A, F, L, O, Q1,and Q4 while the married teachers differed significantly on factors A, C, F, L, and Q from the general population. Fewer score on factor O and Q4 were shown by the unmarried female teachers. Married female teachers were less stable and frustrated. Female teachers (married or unmarried) were found to be significantly higher on factors L Q1. It means that they were more suspicious and self-opinionated. These were significant on factors A and F from general population. Thus, they are reserved, critical, cool, detached, rigid, and aloof respectively.

Lokesh koul (1974) found that the attitude of school teachers towards teaching was positively related to factors A (reserved vs. outgoing) and H (shy vs. venturesome). On the other hand attitude scores of school teachers were found to be related negatively to factors F (sober vs. happy-go-luckey), O (placid vs., apprehensive) and Q4 (relaxed vs. tense).

The major objective of the study conducted by Singh (1974) was to examine the relationship between some personality variables and teaching effectiveness. He found that the needs of superior, average, and inferior teachers were clearly distinct from each other end superior teachers were distinct from the other two in the needs viz. cognition, dominance, autonomy and construction.

Sharma (1974) conducted an investigation into the relationship between personality factors and teaching effectiveness. The sample consisted of 175 B.Ed. students of both the sexes. Cattelle's 16-PF test was administered on the sample for the collection of data. The researcher found 6 factors out of 16 which are positively correlated with teaching effectiveness. These factors were intelligence, trusting, experimenting self-sufficiency. Happy-go-lucky nature and practical mildness. Intelligence came out to be a very important factor for teaching effectiveness. Total personality of the teacher played an important role in teaching effectiveness. Prominent sex differences were also found in the teaching effectiveness.

Gupta (1975) applied Cattle's 16-PF test to predict teacher effectiveness through the use of a personality test. Three hundred male high school teachers having five to six years of teaching experience, 25 principles and 350 students formed the sample. Other tools used were teachers rating scale and pupils rating scale respectively. The researcher notice that highly effective teachers were more effecto-thymic (A+), more intelligence (B+), having more ego-strength (C+), more sergeant (F+), more self-sentiment, (Q#+) and were less guilt prone, less suspicious (O) comparison to the general adult population. Less effective teachers were less intelligent (B_) with lower self-concept control (Q3_) as compared to the general population. Highly effective teachers were significantly more intelligent (B+), emotionally stable (C+) assertive (E+), conscientious (G-), adventurous (H+), tender minded (I+), with higher self-concept (Q3+) and were more warm hearted (A+) in comparison to the less effective teachers. The average effective teachers were more outgoing (A+) sergeant and happy-go-lucky (F+) controlled and socially precise in comparison to the less effective teachers.

Malhotra (1976) in his multistage randomised cluster design showed that poorly adjusted teachers were more direct in their classroom behaviour than teachers who were well adjusted. Mathew George (1976) concluded that there was no significant relationship between creative teacher's personality and indirect/direct behaviour of teachers. And there was positive correlation between creative teacher's personality and 'teacher talk' and negative correlation between creative teacher personality and other dimensions of teacher behaviour.

Grewal (1976) reported that teacher effectiveness was significantly related to some of the personality traits of the teachers. Gupta (1976) reported that the high effective teachers differed significantly from the general population with respect to nine personality factors out of sixteen. They were A+, B+, C+, F+, Q+, Q3, L, O, and Q1.

Gupta (1977) conducted a study regarding the personality structure of primary upper primary school teachers. Eighty five teachers constituted the sample. The age range was 23 years to 38 years. Cattle's 16PF test was used. Means, standard deviations were calculated for each factor in terms of stens and raw scores. The study showed that the primary schools teachers were humble (E_), sober (F_), tender minded and forth righteousness are associated with submissiveness. Day dreaming and feminity, simple and sophisticated nature. They have control over emotions and general behaviour. In fact the primary school teachers who were facing the bare necessities of daily life cannot help but be submissive, day dreaming and unsophisticated in this materialistic age.

Gupta (1977) performed a study on the personality characteristics, adjustment level, academic achievement and professional attitudes of successful teachers. The study intended to find out the personality traits of successful teachers and differentiate them from less successful teachers. It was found that teaching success was significantly related to the factors, A, B, C F, G, H, I, L, N, O, Q3, and Q4 of personality. The researcher also noticed that successful and less successful teachers were different in personality characteristics; adjustment and attitude towards teaching. The personality factor as a group was better indicators of teacher's success than individual factors.

Singh (1978) found out the relationship of teacher's personality. Success in teaching and impact on student's behaviour. He took a sample of 135 male and female teachers with minimum of 3 years experience and 2879 boys of class IX. The tools administered were rating scales, information schedule, critical incidents blank, 16 personality questionnaire, and incomplete sentence blank and Rorschach ink blot test. His study revealed that the theoretical and social values were positively related to teaching success but the economic and aesthetic values were negatively related. Highly successful teachers were better adjusted than that of average and low teachers. Highly successful teachers possess better intellectual capacity and were able to induce learning, develop interest. etc.

Singh (1978) worked on the leadership behaviour of the heads of secondary schools in Haryana. He compared the headmasters' leadership behaviour with that of some other professional leaders and noted the relationship of variables such as personality factors, sex, age, teaching and administrative experience with leadership. Five teachers from each of 100 schools of Haryana state were selected. Thus 100 heads as known by their 500 teachers constituted the sample. 7 factory managers, 7army officers, 7college principals and 7 municipal committee presidents were included in the sample for the study of leadership. The study tools were the leadership behaviour description questionnaire and Cattelles 16 personality factors inventory, it was found that the leadership behaviour was significantly related to the four personality factors i.e. outgoingness, intelligence, emotional stability, and assertiveness. Headmasters were on the 3rd position in the leadership scale out of 5 professional leaders. The head's leadership behaviour was not related to his age. Post-graduate heads were significantly better than graduate heads but total leadership behaviour was neither related to academic qualifications nor related to their teacher experience.

Mishra (1979) conducted a study to know the personality traits of fluent teachers. He measured the fluency of teacher's through Mehdi's test of verbal creativity. Subjects scoring more than 50 were labelled as HFT (highly fluent teachers). The LFT (low fluent teachers) had a score less than 34. These HFT and LFT groups were given Cattelles 16PF test form-A to measure the 16 independent variables of personality. Differences at .05 levels were observed on five personality dimensions. Those are affected by feeling vs. emotionally stable. Sober vs. happy go lucky, shy vs. venturesome, tough-minded vs.tenderminded and conservatives vs. experimenting respectively.

Sharma (1979) observed verbal classroom behaviour of high school science teachers of Uttar Pradesh using Flanders interaction analysis category system (FIACS). He found that structuring the learning had a significant positive relationship with some personality components like general activities, restraint, ascendance, emotional stability, objectivity, thoughtfulness and personal relations. Adaval (1979) observed that harmoniously developed and balanced personality was helpful for success in teaching.

Thakur (1980) made a study on personality characteristics of teachers showing direct and verbal behaviour. He found that there was no significant difference in the teaching behaviour of the direct/indirect teachers due to the variables of age, sex, and experience. Four personality factors namely, C, O, Q3, and Q4 differentiated the direct and indirect teachers significantly.

Singh (1980) investigated on sex role preference in children that is between boys and girls, upper caste and lower caste and role of personality of parents in the developments of sex-role preferences in their children by taking sample of 325 children and parents. The tools administrated were I.T.Scale, A.S. Scale and A.S. Scale. His study revealed that 5 year girls and boys are most feminine and masculine than 3 year old girls and boys. Upper caste children are more conscious of their appropriate sex role than lower castes children. If father dominates, boys dominate, mother dominates, girls play masculine role. That means as variable showed significant effect upon the development of sex role preference in children.

The major aim of Bali's (1981) study was to investigate common personality factors of highly creative persons in different field's viz., poetry, painting, science music etc. the sample consisted of 20 persons who have been awarded or recognised in their fields. They were administrated Cattell's 16 PF test Form-A. The findings were scientists profiles consisted of common factors of ego-ideal, emotional introversion and social will.

Gupta (1981) made a comparative study of the scores of male and female teachers in the inventory of values, personality needs and moral judgement and scores of teachers belonging to different localities (rural and urban). The major findings were: 1. Male and female teachers expressed high preference for the theoretical value and affiliation. The teachers of both sexes expressed keen moral sense. 2 .Urban male teachers were more moral than rural. 3. Urban female teacher's preferred economic and social values. 4. Teachers who were above 45 years preferred the needs of achievement, change and order. Teachers below 30 years had the need of affiliation. 5. Achievement and moral Judgment was the dominant factors in the personality of male and female teachers.

Suthar (1981) studied classroom behaviour of teacher trainees in the context of some personality variables. He reported that 1. There was no significant difference in the classroom behaviour of emotional and tough teacher-trainees except in the case of I/D which was found to be significant at 0.05 levels in favour of emotional teacher trainees, 2. The difference in the mean i/d ratio of extrovert and introvert teacher-trainees was significant at 0.05 levels and it was in favour of extrovert teacher-trainees 3. out of the twelve groups of teacher trainees, ten groups namely emotional, mature, sensitive, confident, insecure, experimenting, extrovert, introvert, submissive and dominating showed indirect influence while the remaining two groups tough and conservative, showed direct influence.

Bhagoli (1982) made an extensive study on "personality characteristics associated with teaching effectiveness seen through Rorschach technique". The sample was 264 teachers

(120males and 144 females). The finding of the study was 1. More effective teachers characterised by their superiority over less effective with respect to their overall intellectual level. 2. More effective teachers were characterised by having more of creative potential indicted by imaginable resources. Inner control was better in these teachers and these people were having fairly higher level of differentiation and integrating in their cognitive and perceptional functioning

Patnaik and panda (1982) made a research on the personality and attitude patterns of good and poor teachers working in secondary schools. 35 good male and 25 good females, 35 poor male and 25 poor female teachers were selected as the sample. The instrument administered were 16 PF –form-C and teacher attitude inventory developed by Ahluwalia (1976). Males have more favourable attitude towards teaching professions, classroom teaching, child centered practices etc. poor female teachers showed favourable attitude towards teaching profession than poor male teachers. Poor male teachers have significantly positive favourable attitude than the poor female teachers.

Rama Chandra Reddy (1982) used Guilford's STDCR personality inventory to measure social extraversion-introversion on the 116 high school science teachers. He selected 15 social extroverts and 17 social introverts for classroom observation. He found that there was highly significant difference at 0.01 levels between the total interaction patterns for the social extrovert and social introvert teachers.

Kamala Chopra (1983) designed her study to identify the personality characteristics related to effective and ineffective teaching. 120 teachers were selected at random (49-effective, 19-average, 52-ineffective teachers) and measured with teacher effective scales used by Pramod Kumar and Mutta. 16PF questionnaire was also administered. The difference in personality traits of the teachers were significant incase of factors A, B, C, Q3, andQ4. However the difference was not statistically significant in case of factors F, G, I, L,

O, Q2. Results showed that effective teachers were significantly more warm hearted and good natured. Those results were in agreement with the findings of Chayya (1974) who observed that the effective teachers were emotionally more stable than the ineffective teachers and Gupta (1976) who observed that the effective teachers differed significantly from the general population on nine personality characteristics.

Rama Mishra (1984) found that the relationship between professional attitude and personality adjustment (r-0.49 of 200 secondary school teachers of Indore city was significant at 0.01 level. If a teacher had positive professional attitude then his personality adjustment was also good.

Peters and Williams (1985) observed that teacher's intellectual disposition did not interact with complexity in the student's performance and that neither student intellectual disposition nor the individual teacher had effect on student performance.

Verma and Sushilas Devi (1987) studied on personality traits and job satisfaction of secondary school teachers by using 16-PF Cattelles questionnaire and teacher job satisfaction questionnaire to 20 secondary school teachers. They found significant difference between more liked and disliked teachers in the 'Y' value of fourth personality factor i.e. (subduedness verses independence) most liked teachers appear to person the trait of independence.

Sundararaja, Sakthivel and Ponnalagappan (1988) showed that the women B.Ed. student-teachers had a more favourable attitude towards teaching than the men student teachers. Nellaippan (1988) reported that men and women teachers differed significantly in their perceptions of many components of effective teaching.

## Research Reviews on Career Choice and Other Works

Eva Schmitt-Rodermund (1991) worked on adolescents career choices in east and west Germany after reunification found that a sample of East and West German adolescents who had made career decisions were drawn from the data collected in 1991, 1996 and in 1998 for the East only. Focusing on gender typicality of career choice. The level of East and West differences that were awaited in 1991, particularly for female adolescents, was expected to be lower in 1996. Overall, due to ongoing economic and social changes, male adolescents were expected to show increased interest in gender neutral occupations, such as trade and commerce. And female adolescents an increasing concentration into female typical occupational areas, such as health services. This trend found in the West but not in the East until 1998.

Yvette Aqui (1994) worked on cognitive and motivational characteristics of adolescents gifted in mathematics comparisons among students with different types of giftedness.

Although numerous studies have compared cognitive and motional characteristics between gifted versus non-gifted students, research comparing those characteristics among different types of gifted students has not kept up with the theoretical development that saw a transition from one-dimensional to multidimensional conceptualisation of giftedness. This study compares cognitive and motivational characteristics of high school students who are academically gifted in math, creatively talented in math, and non-gifted. Whereas no differences were found among the three groups in their beliefs about ability, most of the other characteristics examined in the study distinguished the three groups. Academically gifted female students reported expending more effort than non-academically gifted male students. Creatively talented males put for the more effort cognitive strategies than the academically gifted. Overall , students who were either academically gifted or creatively talented in mathematics perceived that they were self-efficacious in general used cognitive strategies, perceived their math ability and math self-efficacy to be high, and valued learning math more so than their non-gifted age peers.

Philip .M. Wilson (1999) A study on a job seeking self-efficacy scale for people with physical disabilities preliminary development and psychometric testing reveals the both bivariate and multiple regression analysis indicated the global PWES scores had a limited association with leisure time physical activity.($R^2$ adj= .01) sequential regression analysis supported a weak association between physical activity incorporated in the workplace and PWES ($R^2$ adj=.04) and the partial mediation of self-efficacy on the relationship between PWES and workplace physical activity (variance accounted for reduced to $R^2$ adj=.02 when self-efficacy was controlled).

Overall conclusion is the results of the present investigation indicated that self-efficacy acted as a partial mediator of the relationship between perceived environment and workplace physical activity participation. Implications of the findings for physical; activity promoting using ecological – based approaches and future directions for research from this perceptive in working settings are discussed.

Tricia R Prodaniuk, Ronald C Plotnikoff, John C Spence, Phillip M Wilson studied (2003) on the influence of self-efficacy and outcome expectations on the relationship between perceived environment and physical activity in the workplace.

The results reveal that ecological approaches may be particularly useful for understanding and promoting physical activity participation in various settings including the workplace. Yet within the physical activity domain there is a lack of understanding if how ecological environment factors influence behaviour. Thus, the purpose of this study was to examine the relationships between perceived environment, social-cognitive variable, and physical activity behaviour.

D.A Adeyemo and Bola Ogunyemi (2003) conducted research on emotional intelligence and self-efficacy predictors of occupational stress amusing academic staff in Nigerian university.

The study seeks to explain the interactive and relative effects of emotional intelligence and self-efficacy on occupational stress of university academic staff. The results indicated that the two independent variables when taken together were effective in predicting of occupational stress with self-efficacy making higher contribution to the prediction of occupational stress. On the basis of this finding, it is suggested that emotional intelligence programming and self-efficacy intervention techniques will benefit teachers immensely in coping with stress.

Hartsfield, Michael Kirk (2003) conducted research on the internal dynamics of transformational leadership effects of spiritually, emotional intelligence, and self-efficacy. This research broadens the study of transformational leadership beyond the four I's to determine the underlying internal driving forces at work in the transformational leader. The effect that three predictor variables- spirituality, emotional intelligence and self-efficacy have on transformational leadership. Analysis of this data showed emotional intelligence to be the strongest predictor variable followed by self-efficacy and then spirituality.

Chan D. W. (2003) studied on multiple intelligences and perceived self-efficacy among Chinese secondary teachers in Hong Kong.

This study assessed multiple intelligences in a sample of 96 Chinese. Secondary school teachers in Hong Kong, and explored the consistency between these teachers multiple intelligences and their areas of responsibility. Teachers typically reported relative strengths in interpersonal and intrapersonal intelligences and weaknesses in visual, spatial and bodily–kinesthetic intelligences. While there were no gender or age group differences, arts, music, sports teachers indicted greater in strengths in musical intelligence when compared with language and social studies teachers, and guidance teachers indicated greater strengths in both interpersonal and intrapersonal intelligence than did non guidance teachers. Using the eight intelligence as predictors, teacher's intrapersonal intelligence was the significant predictor of their self-efficacy in helping others. The implications of these findings are discussed in light of the current Hong Kong education reform movement and the inadequacy of teacher education.

Todd J. Maurer (2005) worked on career-relevant learning and development, worker age, and beliefs about self-efficacy for development. The study explores an important and under recognised factor that may contribute to this age effect. A decline in self-confidence (self-efficacy) for career relevant learning and skill development with age. The review explores various factors in an organisational setting which might lead to reduced self-confidence for learning. And subsequent lower participation in learning and developmental activities.

Lachman ME, Jelalian E (2006) worked on self-efficacy and attributions for intellectual performance in young and elderly adults.

This study examined subjective assessments of intellectual performance in young (M age=19.46) and elderly (M age=75.13) adults. Male and female college students (n=37) and senior citizens (n=48) were asked to predict their performance before and after taking fluid and crystallised intelligence tests of two trials participants also made causal attributions for their test performance. Elderly participants scored significantly higher on the crystallised test and young participants scored higher on the fluids test. Men's and women's actual performance did not differ, but the elderly women made lower performance predictions on the fluid test than the elderly men. But both the young and elderly groups were more accurate in predicting their test performance for the test on which their performance was higher. Accuracy of performance predictions improved across the two trials. Both age groups were more likely to attribute successful performance to ability and unsuccessful performance to task difficulty.

From the above studies we can observe that a number of factors are responsible for the development of integrated personality among people.

# CHAPTER 3 STATEMENT OF THE PROBLEM

In the present chapter the researcher has stated the problem, enlightened the significance of the problem, enlisted the objectives, framed the hypothesis, and explained the variables of the study.

## Statement of the Problem

"Self-efficacy in relation to intelligence, personality and occupational choice among intermediate students"

## Significance of the Problem

"There is only one success- to be able to spend your life in your own way." *-Christopher Morley*

In today's world, which is marked by competition, it is imperative to manage the stress and strain to keep pace with demands of the society, changing trends, and great expectations. Because only that individual who is successful in all aspects, is the survival of the fittest in this world. Educational field is also not an exception, as globalisation poses a number of challenges.

Present educational system has failed to bring an all round development in the individual. It may be because of faulty examination oriented education, which compels the students to mug up the stereotype questions and answers and just present as it is in examinations without any thought and insight into the subject matter. It is laying more emphasis on the knowledge and information aspect. Our educational system has literally failed to develop life skills which are essential for future of the student. Lack of proper guidance at different stages left child confused. Overburdened curriculum, corporate educational system, great expectations of the teachers and parents is making the children more stress prone and leading to more psychological problems, insecurity , negative competitions , and developing suicidal tendencies among school and college students. Students due to the lack of proper guidance and awareness at intermediate level are opting for stereotype jobs or jobs of their peer choice and lamenting over their choice later which has resulted in job dissatisfaction, maladjustment and inability to cope up with arising needs.

Students success in life depends upon their intelligence bestowed through their heredity, the personality traits they have acquired through their environment (family, school, peer, neighbours, and physical environment) child rearing practices (discipline, instructions given ,guidance provided, facilities provided, physical and psychological need satisfaction),their personality traits, and personal experiences.

Real contentment in life could be achieved only by having faith in ones abilities, purposeful thought and reasoning, taking right decision at right time and optimistic attitude in life.

Present study is significant as it through light on the self-efficacy believes in the intermediate students their personality traits, their intelligence and its influence on their occupational choice.

There is a growing body of evidence that human accomplishments and positive well-being require an optimistic sense of personal efficacy. This is because ordinary social realities are strewn with difficulties. They are full of impediments, adversities, setbacks, frustrations, and inequities. People must have a robust sense of personal efficacy to sustain the perseverant effort needed to succeed.

In pursuits strewn with obstacles, realists either forsake them, abort their efforts prematurely when difficulties arise or become cynical about the prospects of effecting significant changes.

It is widely believed that misjudgment breeds personal problems. Certainly, gross miscalculation can get one into trouble. However, the functional value of accurate self-appraisal depends on the nature of the activity. Activities in which mistakes can produce costly or injurious consequences call for accurate self-appraisal of capabilities. It is a different matter where difficult accomplishments can produce substantial personal and social benefits and the costs involve one's time, and expendable resources. People with high sense of efficacy have the staying power to endure the obstacles and set backs that characterise difficult undertakings.

When people err in their self appraisal they tend to overestimate their capabilities. Their is a benefit rather than a cognitive failing to be eradicated. If efficacy beliefs always reflected only what people can do routinely they would rarely fail but they would not set aspirations beyond their immediate reach nor Mount the extra effort needed to surpass their ordinary performances. In sum, the successful, the venturesome, the sociable, the non- anxious, the non-depressed, the social reformers, and the innovators take an optimistic view of their personal capabilities to exercise influence over events that affect their lives. If not unrealistically exaggerated, such self beliefs foster positive well-being and human accomplishments.

Many of the challenges of life are group problems requiring collective effort to produce significant change. The strength of groups, organisations, and even nations lies partly in people's sense of collective efficacy that they can solve the problems they face and improve their lives through unified effort. People's beliefs in their collective efficacy influence what they choose to do as a group, how much effort they put into it, their endurance when collective efforts fail to produce quick results, and their likelihood of success.

The need of the hour is to boost up self-efficacy beliefs, build up self-confidence, and guide the students in right path by developing good communicative skills, hard working nature, with positive attitude in life.

Keeping in view the existing challenges of education and problems of education the researcher has selected the topic "self-efficacy in relation to intelligence, personality and occupational choice among intermediate students" to contribute for constructive changes in educational system.

## Objectives of the Study

The researcher has undertaken the research with the following objectives and to know the relationship between the following variables of the study.

1. To know the relationship between self efficacy and intelligence.
2. To know the relationship between self-efficacy and personality factors.
3. To know the significance difference of high or low self efficacy on 16-personality factors.
4. To know the significance difference of high or low intelligence on 16-personality factors.
5. To know the effect of gender on self-efficacy.
6. To know the effect of nativity on self-efficacy.
7. To know the effect of parents educational qualifications on self-efficacy.
8. To know the effect of type of the college on self-efficacy.
9. To know the effect of group (subject) on self-efficacy.
10. To know the effect of gender on intelligence.
11. To know the effect of nativity on intelligence.
12. To know the effect of parents educational qualifications on intelligence.

13. To know the effect of type of the college on intelligence.
14. To know the effect of group (subject) on intelligence.
15. To know the effect of demographical variables on personality factor-A (Aloof or warm and outgoing)
16. To know the effect of demographical variables on personality factor-B (Dull or Bright)
17. To know the effect of demographical variables on personality factor-C (Emotional or Mature)
18. To know the effect of demographical factors on personality factor-E (Submissive or dominant)
19. To the know the effect of demographical variables on personality factor-F (Glum, silent or enthusiastic)
20. To the effect of demographical variables on personality factor-G (Casual or conscientious)
21. To the effect of demographical variables on personality factor-H (Timid or adventurous)
22. To the effect of demographical variables on personality factor- I (Tough or sensitive)
23. To know the effect of demographical variables on personality factor-L (Trustful or suspecting)
24. To know the effect of demographical variables on personality factor-M (Conventional or eccentric)
25. To know the effect of demographical variables on personality factor-N (Simple or sophisticated)
26. To know the effect of demographical variables on personality factor-O (Confident or Insecure)
27. To know the effect of demographical variables on personality factor-Q1 (Conservative or Experimenting)
28. To know the effect of demographical variables on personality factor-Q2 (Dependant or self sufficient)
29. To know the effect of demographical variables on personality factor-Q3 (Uncontrolled or self-controlled)
30. To know the effect of demographical variables on personality factor-Q4 (Stable or tense)

31. To know the effect of gender on first occupational choice.
32. To know the effect of nativity on first occupational choice.
33. To know the effect of parents educational qualifications on first occupational choice.
34. To know the effect of type of the college on first occupational choice.
35. To know the effect of group (subject) on first occupational choice.
36. To know the effect of gender on second occupational choice.
37. To know the effect of nativity on the second occupational choice.
38. To know the effect of parents educational qualifications on second occupational choice.
39. To know the effect of type of the college on second occupational choice.
40. To know the effect of group on second occupational choice.

## Hypotheses of the Study

1. There is no significant relationship between self-efficacy and intelligence
2. There is no significant relationship between self-efficacy and personality factors.
3. There is no significant difference of high or low self-efficacy on personality factors.
4. There is no significant difference of high or low intelligence on 16-personality factors.
5. There is no significant effect of gender on self-efficacy.
6. There is no significant effect of nativity on self-efficacy.
7. There is no significant effect of parent's educational qualifications on self-efficacy.
8. There is no significant effect of type of the college on self-efficacy.

9. There is no significant effect of group (subject) on self-efficacy.
10. There is no significant effect of gender on intelligence.
11. There is no significant effect of nativity on intelligence.
12. There is no significant effect of parent's educational qualifications on intelligence.
13. There is no significant effect of type of the college on intelligence.
14. There is no significant effect of group (subject) on intelligence.
15. There is no significant effect of demographical variables on personality factor-A (Aloof or warm and outgoing)
16. There is no significant effect of demographical variables on personality factor-B (Dull or bright)
17. There is no significant effect of demographical variables on personality factor-C (Emotional or mature)
18. There is no significant effect of demographical variables on personality factor-E (Submissive or dominant)
19. There is no significant effect of demographical variables on personality factor-F (Glum, silent or enthusiastic)
20. There is no significant effect of demographical variables on personality factor-G (Casual or conscientious)
21. There is no significant effect of demographical variables on personality factor-H (Timid or adventurous)
22. There is no significant effect of demographical variables on personality factor-I (Tough or Sensitive)
23. There is no significant effect of demographical variables on personality factor-L (Trustful or suspecting)

24. There is no significant effect of demographical variables on personality factor-M (Conventional or eccentric)
25. There is no significant effect of demographical variables on personality factor-N (simple or sophisticated)
26. There is no significant effect of demographical variables on personality factor-O (Confident or insecure)
27. There is no significant effect of demographical variables on personality factor-Q1 (Conservative or experimenting)
28. There is no significant effect of demographical variables on personality factor-Q2 (Dependent or sufficient)
29. There is no significant effect of demographical variables on personality factor-Q3 (Uncontrolled or self-controlled)
30. There is no significant effect of demographical variables on personality factor-Q4 (Stable or tense)
31. There is no significant effect of gender on first occupational choice.
32. There is no significant effect of nativity on first occupational choice.
33. There is no significant effect of parent's educational qualifications on first occupational choice.
34. There is no significant effect of type of the college on first occupational choice.
35. There is no significant effect of group (subject) on first occupational choice.
36. There is no significant effect of gender of second occupational choice.
37. There is no significant effect of nativity on second occupational choice.
38. There is no significant effect of parent's educational choice on second occupational choice.

39. There is no significant effect of type of the college on second occupational choice.
40. There is no significant effect of group (subject) on second occupational choice.

## Variables of the Study

**(*a*) Self Efficacy:** it is the belief in one's capability to organise and execute the course of action required to manage prospective situations.

**(*b*) Intelligence:** it is the aggregate of global capacity of the individual to act purposefully, to think rationally and to deal effectively with his environment-Wechsler.

Intelligence is the ability to undertake activities that are characterised by {1} difficulty {2} complexity {3} abstraction {4} economy {5} adaptiveness to a goal {6}social, value {7} and the emergence of the originals, and to maintain such activities under conditions that demand a consideration of energy and resistance to emotional force-Stoddard.

Terman defining intelligence says "an individual is intelligent in proportion as he is able to carry on abstract thinking. Intelligence, the dictionary says, is "The capacity to acquire and apply knowledge."

**(*c*) Personality**: All port says "Personality is the dynamic organisation within the individual of those psychophysical systems that determine his unique adjustment to his environment".

Warren's dictionary defines personality, "personality is the integrative organisation of all the cognitive, affective, con-native and physical characteristics of an individual as it manifests itself in focal distinction from others".

Mark Sherman says "personality is the characteristic pattern of behaviours, cognitions, and emotion which may be experienced by the individual and manifest to others".

Freedenberg "personality is a stable system of complex characteristics by which the life pattern of the individual may be identified".

***(d)* Occupational Choice**: It is conscious choice of an occupation based on truthful analysis of ones own personality, his likes and dislikes his special aptitudes, and his handicaps to arouse his latent talents.

**Sex**: Girls and boys studying in Intermediate colleges.

**Locality** or nativity here means Rural intermediate students of countryside. Urban intermediate students of city municipality.

***(g)* Parent's educational qualification**: includes illiterates, ssc, and intermediate, graduation, and post graduation.

***(h)* Type of the college:** here it means Government College, Aided College, Unaided College, and Minority College.

***(i)* Group:** The students studying in intermediate colleges are divided into four groups. They are

Mathematics physics and chemistry (MPC)

Biological science physics and chemistry (BPC)

History economics and civics (HEC)

Commerce economics and civics (CEC)

# METHOD OF INVESTIGATION

In the preceding chapter, the researcher has presented the review of related literature, focused the problem, discussed the significance of the problem, stated the objectives, and formulated the hypotheses.

In the present chapter discussion about the methodology of the research is proposed to be presented. This chapter discusses about the design of the study, sample considered, tools used, the methods followed for data collection and the statistical techniques adopted.

The research is intended to find out the relation between the following variables.

1. Self-efficacy, intelligence, personality, and occupational choice.
2. To find out the effect of the demographical factors on self-efficacy, intelligence, personality and occupational choice.

## Design of the Study

The researcher has selected four variables for the study. Self-efficacy and occupational choice as dependent variables and intelligence and personality are independent variables, apart from gender, nativity, parents educational qualifications, type of the college, and group (subject).are also independent variables. As the number of independent variables are more multiple regression analysis was employed to test the hypothesis formulated in the present investigation apart from significance of difference.

## Sample of the Study

Nine hundred intermediate students (both girls and boys) studying in different colleges at Kurnool District constituted the sample of the study. First the number of colleges in Kurnool District were listed. Through stratified random sampling in total sixteen colleges were selected of which four are Government Institutions, Four aided Institutions, four unaided Institutions and Four minority Institutions.

From each type 225 students of which 100 are boys and 125 are girls. Thus the total of 900 students of which 400 are boys and 500 are girls were selected which constitute the sample of present study.

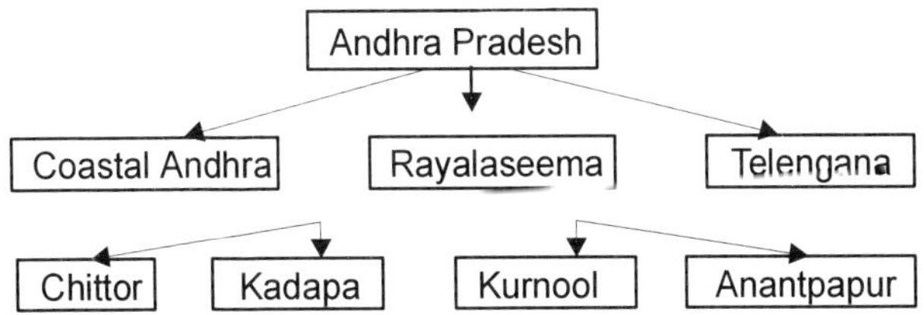


**Table 4.1. Showing Number of Intermediate Colleges Selected For Study**

| Sl.No. | Type of the college | Number |
|---|---|---|
| 1. | Government | 4 |
| 2. | Aided | 4 |
| 3. | Un-aided | 4 |
| 4. | minority | 4 |

**Table 4.2. Showing Total Sample of the Study**

| S.No | Type of the college | Number of boys | Number of girls | Total sample |
|---|---|---|---|---|
| 1. | government | 100 | 125 | 225 |
| 2. | aided | 100 | 125 | 225 |
| 3. | un-aided | 100 | 125 | 225 |
| 4. | minority | 100 | 125 | 225 |
| 5. | total | 400 | 500 | 900 |

## Tools Used

In this study the researcher has used the following tools.

1. **Self-efficacy scale** by Ralf Schwarzer & Matthias Jerusalem, 1993.

2. **Standard Progressive Matrices** (sets-A, B, C, D and E) by J.C.Raven 1958

3. **16-personality factor questionnaire** by Cattele (form-C) 1962.

4. **Occupational choice** (locally standardised)

## DESCRIPTION OF TOOL

### Self-efficacy Scale

### Definitions

Self-efficacy is belief in one's capability to organize and execute the course of action required to manage prospective situation. It is concerned with individual's perceived capabilities to produce results and to attain designated types of performance. Self-efficacy judgments are both task and situation-specific, contextual .individual makes use of these judgments in reference to some type of goal.

Self-efficacy beliefs develop from various sources like mastery experience, verbal persuasions, vicarious experiences etc. physiological states such as anxiety, stress, arousal, fatigue and mood states also provide information about efficacy beliefs.

It is important to restate that these sources of efficacy information are not directly translated into judgments of competence. Individuals interpret the results of events, and these interpretations provide the information on which judgments are based. The types of information people attend to and use to make efficacy judgments, and the rules they employ for weighting and integrating them, form the basis for such interpretations. Thus, the selection, integration, interpretation, and recollection of information influence judgments of self-efficacy.

## Importance of Self Efficacy In Daily Life

Self efficacy beliefs influence motivational and self-regulatory process in several ways. They influence the choices people make and the courses of action they pursue. Strong self-efficacy beliefs enhance human accomplishment and personal well-being in many ways. People with a strong sense of personal competence in a domain approach difficult tasks in that domain as challenges to be mastered rather than as dangers to be avoided, have greater intrinsic interest in activities, set challenging goals and maintain a strong commitment to them, heighten their efforts in the face of failure, more easily recover their confidence after failures or setbacks and attribute failure to insufficient effort or deficient knowledge and skills which they believe they are capable of acquiring. High self-efficacy helps create feelings of serenity in approaching difficult tasks and activities. Conversely, people with low self-efficacy may believe that things are tougher than they really are, a belief that fosters stress, depression, and a narrow vision of how best to solve a problem. As a result of these influence, self-efficacy beliefs are strong determinants and predictors of the level of accomplishment that individuals finally attain.

## Example of Self Efficacy

Students confident in their academic skills expect high marks on exams and expect the quality of their work to reap benefits. The opposite is also true of those who lack such confidence. Students who doubt their academic ability envision low marks before they begin an exam. The expected results of these imagined performances will be differently envisioned continued good grades and academic success for the former, curtailed possibilities and academic failure for the latter.

The socially anxious man confronted with the decision of whether to attend the party envisions disastrous outcomes largely because he has little confidence in his capabilities to meet the demands associated with parties. These beliefs vary in level, strength, and generality and these dimensions prove important in determining appropriate measurements.

## Measurement of Self Efficacy

Self-efficacy beliefs should be measured in terms of particularised judgments of capability that may vary across realms of activity, different levels of task demands within a given activity, domain, and under different situational circumstances.

The researcher has selected the self-efficacy questionnaire standardised and prepared by Ralf Schwarzer and Matthias Jerusalem, in the year 1993.

Self-efficacy scale consists of ten statements with four options. {1=not at all true, 2=hardly true, 3=moderately true, 4=exactly true.} The student has to go through the statement and give one response of his choice.

## Scoring of Self-efficacy

It consists of ten statements. There are four alternative responses. These responses were numbered 1 to 4 (not at all true-1, hardly true-2, moderately true-3, and exactly true-4). The minimum and maximum possible scores on self efficacy scale ranges from 10-40. Low score indicates low self efficacy high score indicates high self efficacy. The reliability of the scale was established by using test-retest method and it is found to be 0.64 and validity of the scale computed is 0.80.

## Reliability And Validity

The reliability of the self-efficacy questionnaire was established by using test-retest method. The researcher has selected 50 students of intermediate first and second year and administered the self-efficacy questionnaire to them. Again after one month the same questionnaire was given to the same students of intermediate first year and second year and test was administered. Then reliability and validity was found to be root .64 and 0.80. This value show that this scale is suitable for our condition. The same scale is translated into Telugu by the researcher with the help of research supervisor.

## Standard Progressive Matrices

It is a test of person's capacity at the time of the test to apprehend meaningless figures presented for his observation see the relation between them , conceive the nature of the figure completing each system of relations presented ,and by so doing develop a systematic method of reasoning.

Raven's progressive matrices consist of five sets of non-verbal items {A, B, C, and D & E} .The scale consists of 60 problems divided into five sets of 12. In each set the first problem is as nearly as possible self-evident. The problems which follow become progressively difficult. The five sets provide five opportunities for grasping method and five progressive assessments of a person's capacity for intellectual activity. Each set has 12 items in order of difficulty. To ensure sustained interest and freedom from fatigue, the figures in each problem are boldly presented, accurately drawn and, as far as, possible pleasing to look at. The scale is intended to cover the whole range of intellectual development from the time the child is able to grasp the idea of finding a missing piece to complete the pattern and to be sufficiently long to assess a person's maximum capacity to form comparisons reason by analogy without being unduly exhausting or unwieldy.

Everyone whatever his age, is given exactly the same series of problems in the same order and is asked to work at his own speed, without interruption, from the beginning to end of the scale. As the order of the problem provides the standard training in the method of working, the scale can be given either as an individual, a self-administered or as a group test. Person's total scores provide an index of his intellectual capacity, whatever his nationality or education. The contribution which each of the five sets makes to the total provides a means of assessing the consistency of the estimate.

Each problem in the scale is really the mother or source of a system of thought hence the name progressive matrices. The scale has a retest reliability varying with age, from o.83 to0.93. It correlates 0.86 with the Terman-Merril scale. And has been found to have a "g" saturation of 0.82+. A set of test book is required for administration of RPM.

The researcher has selected intermediate first year and second year students for his research work. Hence he made them sit sufficiently apart comfortably at tables with RPM booklets and answer sheets. Necessary instructions were given followed by strict supervision to avoid copying. One hour time was given to solve 60 non-verbal items.

### Scoring of Standard Progressive Matrices

A person's score on the scale is the total number of problems he solves correctly when he is allowed to work quietly through the series from the beginning to the end. Non-verbal responses of standard progressive matrices are scored according to the scoring key prepared by J.C.Raven.

### Sixteen Personality Factor Questionnaire

Growing use of 16-PF form A and B in many studies in clinical, dimensions of personality form-C has been constructed. Form A and Form-B take much time hence form-C has been prepared keeping in view.

1. To meet the need
2. To use at the same time a more elementary vocabulary
3. To include an index
4. To guard against attempt at distortion of the self picture.
5. As a third extension of the 16-PF itself.

In terms of the personality factors measured, form-C is exactly parallel to form- A and form-B. An extensive factor analysis, originally based on many hundreds of new questions, was carried out, as reported in detail elsewhere. It aimed to give maximum reliability and validity of measurement possible with only six items per factor. The result showed good validity and confirmed that the same factors are being measured as in the A and B 16PF forms. It tests the basic independent factors such as emotional stability, dominance, timidity, shrewdness, intelligence, enthusiasm (surgency), conservatism, nervous tension, and the factors involved in neuroticism, morale, leadership, social adjustment, and vocational preference and success.

**Table 4.3 : Showing 16-Personality Factors**

| | | |
|---|---|---|
| FACTOR-A | Aloof(schizothyme) | Warm (cyclothymis) |
| FACTOR-B | Dull (low general ability) | Bright (intelligent) |
| FACTOR-C | Emotional (general ability) | Mature (egocentric) |
| FACTOR-E | Submissive (submission) | Dominant (dominance) |
| FACTOR-F | Glum, silent (desurgency) | Enthusiastic surgency) |
| FACTOR-G | Casual (weakness of character) | Conscientious (super-ego) |
| FACTOR-H | Timid (withdrawn schizothyme) | Adventurous (cyclothymiacs) |
| FACTOR-I | tough | Sensitive |
| FACTOR-L | trustful | Suspecting |
| FACTOR-M | Conventional (concerns) | Eccentric (unconcern) |
| FACTOR-N | simple | Sophisticated |
| FACTOR-O | Confident (freedom from anxiety) | Insecure (anxious insecure) |
| FACTOR-Q1 | conservative | Experimenting |
| FACTOR-Q2 | dependent | Self sufficient |
| FACTOR-Q3 | uncontrolled | Self-controlled |
| FACTOR-Q4 | stable | Tense |

The sixteen dimensions are independent. That is correlation between one and another is usually negligible. And each of the sixteen scales brings an entirely new piece of information about the person, a condition not found in many alleged multi-dimensional scales.

## Capsule Description of Sixteen Personality Factors

Factor-A Aloof (Schizothymia) the person who scores low (1or2) on this factor tends to be stiff, cool aloof. He likes things rather than people. Working alone and avoidance of clash of view points. He is likely to be precise and rigid in his way of doing things and in personal standards, and in many occupations these are desirable traits. He may tend, at time to be critical, obstructive or hard.

Factor –A Warm, outgoing (Cyclothymia) the person who scores high on factor –A tends to be good-natured, easygoing, ready to cooperate, attentive to people, softhearted, kindly, trustful, adaptable. He likes occupations dealing with people and socially impressive situations. He readily forms active group. He is generous in personal relations, less afraid of criticism, better able to remember names of people. But he is often less dependable in precision work and in obligations.

Factor-B Dull (low general ability) the person scoring low on factor-B tends to be slow to learn and grasp, dull sluggish. He tends to have little taste or capacity for the higher forms of knowledge and to be somewhat boorish.

Factor-B Bright (intelligence) the person who scores high on factor-B tends to be quick to grasp ideas, a fast learner, and intelligence. He is usually rather cultured.

Factor-C Emotional(general instability) the person who seeks low on factor-C tends to be emotionally immature, lacking in frustration tolerance, changeable, evasive, neurotically fatigued, worrying, easily annoyed ,generally dissatisfied, having symptoms of phobia, sleep disturbances, psychosomatic complaints. Low factor –score is common to almost all forms of mental disorders.

Factor-C mature (ego strength) the person who scores high on factor-C tends to be emotionally mature, stable, calm, phlegmatic, realistic about life, placid, possessing ego strength, having an integrated philosophy of life, better able to maintain high group morale.

Factor-E submissive (submission) the person who scores low on Factor-E tends to be dependent, a follower, and to take action which goes along with the group. He tends to lean on others in making decisions and is often soft-hearted, expressive and easily upset.

Factor-E Dominant (dominance) the person who scores high on factor-E tends to be ascendant, self-assured, assertive, and independent-minded. Bold in his approach to situations. He may at times be hard, stern, hostile, solemn, tough-minded, and authoritarian.

Factor-F Glum, silent (de-surgency) the person who scores low on factor F tends to be taciturn, reticent introspective. He is some times incommunicative, melancholic. Anxious, depressed, smug, languid, slow.

Factor-F Enthusiastic (surgency) the person who scores high on this trait tends to be cheerful, talkative, frank, expressive, quick, alert, and imperturbable. He is frequently chosen as an elected leader.

Factor –G Casual (weakness of Character the person who scores low on factor-G tends to be fickle, undependable, irresolute, unsteady, quitting, he is sometimes demanding, impatient, indolent, obstructive, lacking to internal standards.

Factor-G Conscientious (super ego strength) the person who scores high on factor-G tends to be strong in charter persevering, responsible, determined, consistent, planful, energetic, cautious, well-organised. He is usually conscientious, with high regard for moral standards, and prefers efficient people to other companions.

Factor-H Timid (withdrawn schizothymia) the person who scores low on this trait tends to be shy, withdrawn, cautious, retiring, cool, a wallflower.

He usually has inferiority feelings. He tends to be slow and impeded in speech and in expressing himself, dislikes occupations with personal contacts, prefers one or two close friends to large groups, and is not able to keep in contact with all that is going on around him.

Factor-H Adventurous (adventurous cyclothymiacs)the person who scores high on factor-H tends to be sociable , participating, ready to try new things, spontaneous, abundant in emotional response. He is able to face wear and tear in dealing with people and grueling emotional situations, without fatigue. However, he can be careless of detail, ignore danger signals, and consume much time talking. He may be pushy and active in interest in the opposite sex.

Factor-I Tough (toughness) the persons who scores low on factor-I tends to be practical, realist. Masculine, independent, responsible, but uncultured. He is sometimes phlegmatic, hard, cynical, and smug. He tends to keep a group operating in a practical and realist no-nonsense basis.

Factor-I Sensitive (sensitivity) the person who scores high on Factor-I tends to be tender-minded, imaginative, introspective, artistic, fastidious, excitable. He is sometimes demanding, impatient, dependent, and impractical; he dislikes crude people and rough occupations. He tends to slow up group performance, and to upset group morale by negative remarks.

Factor-L Trustful (lack of paranoid tendency) the person who scores low on factor-L tends to be free of jealous tendencies, adaptable. Cheerful, composed, concerned about other people, a good team worker.

Factor-L Suspecting (paranoid tendency) the persons who scores high on factor-L tends to be mistrusting and doubtful he is often involved in his own ego is self-opinionated, and interested in internal and mental life. He is usually deliberate in his actions. Unconcerned about other people. And a poor team leader.

Factor-M Conventional (practical concernedness) the person who scores low of factor-M tends to be anxious, to do the right thing. Practical and conformist. He is easily concerned but able to keep his head to emergencies; he is often rather narrowly correct and unimaginative.

Factor-M Eccentric (Bohemian unconcern) the person who scores high in this factor tends to be unconventional, unconcerned, egocentric, sensitive, imaginative, he some times makes emotional scenes, is somewhat responsible, impractical, undependable, he is often rejected in group situations.

Factor-N Simple (Naïve simplicity) the persons who score low in this factor tends to be unsophisticated, sentimental, and simple. He is easily pleased and sometimes crude, and awkward.

Factor-N sophisticated (sophistication) the person who scores high in this factor tends to be polished, experienced, worldly, shrewd, he tends to be hard headed and analytical, he has an intellectual, unsentimental approach to situations.

Factor-O Confident (freedom from anxiety) the person who scores low in this factor tends to be placid, calm, with unshakable nerve, he has a mature, unanxious confidence in himself and his capacity to deal with things, he is resilient and secure.

Factor-O Insecure (anxious insecurity) the person who scores high in this factor tends to be depressed, moody, a worrier. Suspicious, brooding, avoiding people. He has a childlike tendency to anxiety in difficulties. He does not feel accepted in groups or free to participate. High factor-O score is very common in clinical groups of all types.

Factor Q1-Conservative (conservatism) the person who scores low in this factor tends to be overly cautious and moderate. He is opposed to any change, inclined to go along with traditions, and tends not to be interested in analytical intellectual thought.

Factor - Q1Experimenting radicalism) the person who scores high on factorQ1 tends to be interested in intellectual matters and fundamental issues. He frequently takes issue with ideas, either old or new. He tends to be better informed less inclined to moralise. And more inclined to experiment in life generally, more tolerant of inconvenience.

Factor - Q2 Dependent (group dependence) the person s who scores low in this factor tends to be work oriented, and make decisions with other people. Like and depends on social approval and admiration. He tends to go along with the group and may be lacking in resolution.

Factor - Q2 self-sufficient the person who score high in this factor tend to be independent, resolute, accustomed to going his own way, making decisions and taking action on his own. He is not necessarily dominant however in his relations with others.

Factor - Q3 uncontrolled (poor self sentiment) the person who scores low in this factor tends to lack control and character stability he is not too considerate, careful, or conscientious.

Factor Q3 self-controlled (high self-sentiment) the person who scores high in this factor tends to have strong control, of his emotions and general behaviour, is inclined to be considered, careful, and evident what is commonly termed self-respect. He sometimes tends, however to be obstinate. Effective leader are high on Q3.

Factor-Q4 stable (relaxation) the person who scores low on factorQ4 tends to be calm, relaxed, composed and satisfied.

FactorQ4 tense the persons who scores high in this factors tend to be tense, excitable, restless, fretful, impatience. He is often over fatigued, but unable to remain inactive. He takes a poor view of group unity, orderliness, leadership.

## Design and Construction of the Test

**(*a*) Arrangement of items :** Six questions (also called items) are set up for each of the sixteen factors except general intelligence, where eight items are used. To the 98 items thus constituted are added seven motivational distortion items. The items are arranged in a roughly cyclic order determined by a plan to give maximum convenience in scoring by stencil.

**(*b*) Method of answering :** Three alternative answers are provided for each f the 105 items, since the two-alternative forced choice situation, forbidding any middle of the road compromise tends to force an incorrect distribution of attitudes and often produces aversion to the test on the part of the examinee.

**Validity and reliability:** the validity of the test itself is meant to be an internal validity. That is to say, the items, as stated above, are chose as being good measures of the factors, as shown by factor analysis. The mean correlations of all single items with factors they represent is +.37. and the mean correlation of each group of sex items with factor it represents is about +.71.

Reliability has been worked out as a test-retest correlation with a one-week interval between. The values obtained on a population of two hundred students are factor A-.54 B-.57, C-.47, E-.42, F-.50, G-.41,H-.61, I - .55, L-.45, M-.39, N-.41, O-.32, Q1-.71, Q2.45, Q3-.52 Q4 .55 respectively the reliability then range from +.75 to +.90 area for each of the sixteen factor scales. The same scale was translated by Mrs. Gayathri Research Scholar Dept. of Education S.V.U. Tirupati. It is an adopted one.

## Scoring of 16-personality Factors

There are 105 items in 16-personality factors scale. Each item scores 0, 1, or 2. Except the factor-B, intelligence items, which score 0(incorrect) or 1 correct). Each item score contributes to only one factor i.e. an item's score is never added into two different factors, which would produce false correlations between these factors. Scoring is accomplished by key, easily, rapidly, and objectively (in a standard manner). The answers are on separate answer sheet. Card-board stencil scoring keys are used one for factors A, C, F, H, L, N, Q1, andQ3, and the other for B, E, G, I, M, O, Q2, MD and Q4. We must fit the stencil over the answer sheet and count the pencil marks visible through the holes for factor-A, allowing one for holes so marked and 2 for holes with a 2 above them. Sum and enter the total where the spear point indicates the space for–A (raw score) on the right. Same criteria is adopted for factors C and F etc. proceed the same for second stencil. But note the factor B is peculiar in having holes only with a score 0 or 1.

Before using the scoring stencils, the technician should take a quick look at each answer sheet to make sure that there are no anomalous responses. E.g. making two out of three alternatives, or entirely omitting an item.

## Occupational Preference List

Occupational preference list was standardized by research scholar. For this purpose 100 students of intermediate first and second year were selected using random sampling technique. These students are from different groups (MPC,

**Table 4.4. Showing the List of Occupations known at Intermediate Level**

| Sl. No. | MPC/BPC | HEC/CEC |
|---|---|---|
| 1. | Doctor | Lawyer |
| 2. | Engineer | Judge |
| 3. | Astronomer | Journalist |
| 4. | Architect | Collector |
| 5. | Physicst | Politician |
| 6. | Botanist | Author |
| 7. | Physiotherapist | Chartered Accountant |
| 8. | Pharmacist | Bank Cashier |
| 9. | Zoologist | Business Manager |
| 10. | Agriculturist | Accountant |
| 11. | Any Other | Any Other |

BPC, CEC, and HEC). Then they were asked to enlist the professions of their choice based upon their groups. Then 10 common preferences enlisted by 100 students based upon their groups were selected for the large sample. The selected list is as follows.

## Scoring for Occupational Preferences

The students were required to rank the 10 occupations according to their preference the researcher has considered first and second occupational choice for research purpose and omitted remaining preferences.

## Data Collection Procedure

Through stratified random sampling technique researcher has selected intermediate colleges of Kurnool district. The researcher met the sample of 900 students in groups of 20 each. They were distributed self-efficacy questionnaire and RPM. After developing rapport they were explained the significance of the study and instructions were given accordingly.

In second session 16 personality factors and occupational choice list was given and data was collected from all the 900 students. The responses of the subject were scored accordingly and the obtained data was subjected to statistical analysis. Such as t-values MRI.

## Statistical Analysis

The researcher has collected the required data from the sample and, scores were given to each questionnaire as per the scoring key, and correlations, frequency distribution, mean standard deviation, t-values and f-values were computed, for the obtained data.

# RESULTS AND DISCUSSION

Previous Chapters were devoted for the presentation of review of related literature, for focusing the problem, for the discussion of the significance of the study for the formulation of hypothesis, for working out the design of the study, for the selection of the methods of sampling and procedure adopted for data collection.

This chapter discusses the results related to the variables of the study. It mainly presents the results related to the relationship between the selected variables.

Results are presented in the form of means, standard deviation, t-values, F-values, correlations, and MRA.

## Hypothesis-1

"There is no significant relationship between self-efficacy and intelligence."

Results pertaining to this hypothesis are presented in the table 5.1.

**Table 5.1. Showing Co-relation between Self-efficacy and Intellignece**

| Variable | Co-relation |
|---|---|
| Self-efficacy<br>Intelligence(RPM) | .119** |

**significant at 0.01 level.

The calculated correlation value reveals that correlation is significant at 0.01 level for self-efficacy and intelligence. It means self-efficacy and intelligence are positively co-related. Higher the intelligence, higher the self-efficacy is.

Intelligence develops self confidence, and enhances success by developing rationale thought. It helps to adjust in various situations of life.

Hence the hypothesis "there is no significant relationship between self-efficacy and intelligence" is not accepted.

## Hypothesis-2

"There is no significant relationship between self-efficacy and 16-personality factors."

Result pertaining to this hypothesis is presented in table 5.2

**Table 5.2. Showng Corelation between Self-efficacy and 16-Personality Factors (N=900)**

| | Personality factors | Correlation |
|---|---|---|
| Self-efficacy | FA | -.044@ |
| | FB | -.033@ |
| | FC | -.100** |
| | FE | -.060@ |
| | FF | -.043@ |
| | FG | -.027@ |
| | FH | .057@ |
| | FI | -.035@ |
| | FL | .074* |
| | FM | -.007@ |
| | FN | -.070* |
| | FO | -.079* |
| | FQ1 | -.052@ |
| | FQ2 | .143** |
| | FQ3 | -.005@ |
| | FQ4 | .053@ |
| | FTOT | .007@ |

#@ -not significant
#*significant at 0.05 level
#**significant at 0.01 level

**1. Self-efficacy and factor-A :** The calculated correlation value shows that there is no significant correlation between self-efficacy and personality factor-A. (aloofness or warm and outgoing)

**2. Self-efficacy and factor-B :** The calculated correlation value reveals that there is no significant co-relation between self-efficacy and personality factor-B. It means that there is no relation between self-efficacy and being dull (low general ability) or bright (intelligence).

**3. Self efficacy and factor-C :** The calculated co relational value reveals that it is significant for self-efficacy and personality factor-C (at 0.01 level). It means that there is negative correlation between self-efficacy and personality factor-C, that is being emotional (general instability) or being mature (ego strength).

**4. Self-efficacy and personality factor-E :** The calculated corelation value reveals that there is no significant corelation between self-efficacy and personality factor-E. It means that there is no relation between self-efficacy and being submissive or dominant.

**5. Self-efficacy and personality factor-F :** The calculated value shows that there is no significant corelation between self-efficacy and personality factor-F. It means that there is no correlation between self-efficacy and being glum, silent (desurgency) or being enthusiastic (surgency).

**6. Self-efficacy and personality factor-G :** The calculated value shows that there is no significant corelation between self-efficacy and personality factor – G. it means there is no correlation between self-efficacy and being casual (weak of character) or being conscientious (super ego strength).

**7. Self-efficacy and personality factor- H :** The calculated correlation value reveals that there is no significant corelation between self-efficacy and personality factor-H that is being timid (withdrawn schizothyme) or being adventures (cyclothymiacs).

**8. Self-efficacy and personality factor-I :** The calculated correlation value reveals that there is no significant corelation between self-efficacy and personality factor-I that is being tough or being sensitive.

**9. Self-efficacy and personality factor-L :** Calculated corelational value reveals that there is significant positive correlation (significant at .05 levels) between self-efficacy and personality factor-L. It means that there is positive relation between self-efficacy and being trustful or being suspecting.

**10. Self-efficacy and personality factor-M :** The calculated corelational value reveals that there is no significant corelation between self-efficacy and personality factor-M .that is being conventional or being eccentric

**11. Self-efficacy and personality factor-N :** The calculated corelational value reveals that there is significant negative correlation (significant at 0.05 level) between self-efficacy and personality factor-N. i.e. being simpler or being sophisticated.

**12. Self-efficacy and personality factor-O :** The calculated corelational value shows that there is significant negative correlation between self-efficacy and personality factor–O. i.e. being confident (freedom from anxiety) or being insecure (anxious, insecure)

**13. Self-efficacy and personality factor-Q1 :** The calculated corelational value reveals that there is no significant correlation between self-efficacy and personality factorQ1.ie. Being conservative or being experimenting.

**14. Self-efficacy and personality factor Q2 :** The calculated correlation value reveals that there is significant positive correlation (significant at 0.01 levels) between self-efficacy and personality factor Q2 i.e. being dependent or being self-sufficient

**15. Self-efficacy and personality factor-Q3 :** The calculated corelational value reveals that there is no significant corelation between self-efficacy and personality factorQ3 i.e. being uncontrolled or being self controlled.

**16. Self-efficacy and personality factor Q4 :** The calculated correlation value reveals that there is no significant correlation between self-efficacy and personality factor Q4 i.e. Being stable or being tense.

Finally the total corelational values of self-efficacy and 16-personality factors reveal that there is no significant Correlation between self-efficacy and 16-personality factors.

Hence the hypothesis "there is no significant correlation between self-efficacy and 16-personality"factors is accepted.

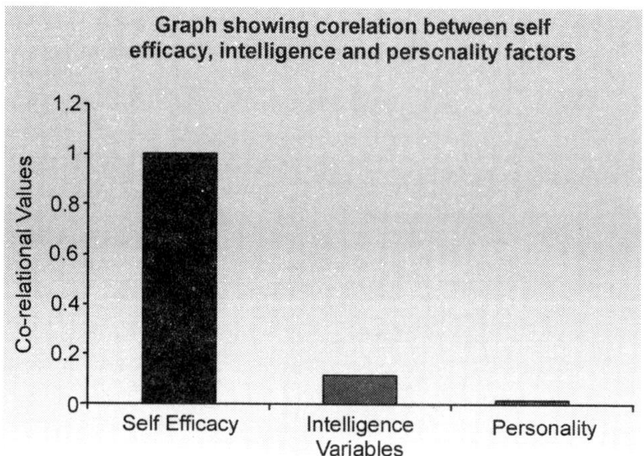


The researcher was interested to find out first and second occupational choice of Arts and Science Students with low self efficacy and high self efficacy. Preference were presented in the form as Tables. Only three choices with high frequency were taken into consideration and remaining choice were omitted.

The calculated frequency values of first occupational choice of Science and Arts students with low self-efficacy reveals that 39.43% of science students have preferred doctor profession, where as Arts students preferred lawyer Profession, 23.98% science students have preferred

**Table 5.3. Showing First Occupational Choice of Students with Low Self-efficacy (N=900)**

| Occupa-tions | Frequ-ency | Cumu-lative-frequency | Percen-tage | Cumulative percentage |
|---|---|---|---|---|
| 1 | 97 | 97 | 39.43 | 39.431 |
| 2 | 59 | 156 | 23.98 | 63.415 |
| 3 | 3 | 159 | 1.22 | 64.634 |
| 4 | 17 | 176 | 6.91 | 71.545 |
| 5 | 4 | 180 | 1.63 | 73.171 |
| 6 | 10 | 190 | 4.07 | 77.236 |
| 7 | 7 | 197 | 2.85 | 80.081 |
| 8 | 6 | 203 | 2.44 | 82.520 |
| 9 | 5 | 208 | 2.03 | 84.553 |
| 10 | 13 | 221 | 5.28 | 89.837 |
| 11 | 25 | 246 | 10.16 | 100.000 |

Engineering profession where as arts students preferred. Lawyer profession and 10.16% science and arts students have preferred other profession than enlisted. Even though they have low self-efficacy they are over ambitious, and lack awareness of their abilities and limitations.

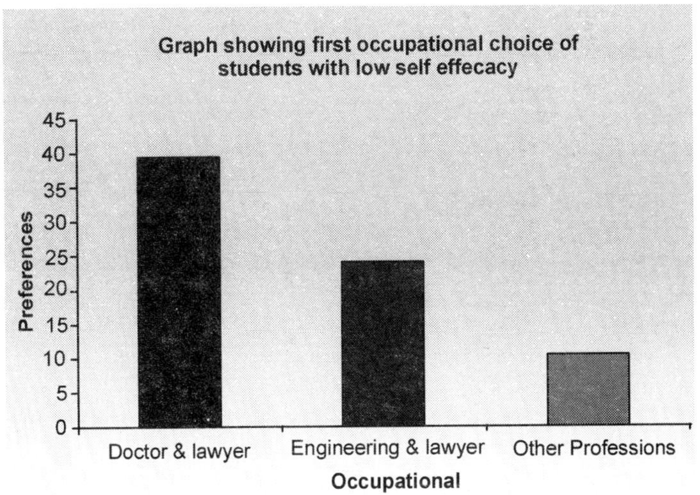

**Table 5.4. Showing Second Occupational Choice of Students with Low Self-Efficacy (N=900)**

| Occupa-tions | Frequ-ency | Cumu-lative-frequency | Percen-tage | Cumulative percentage |
|---|---|---|---|---|
| 0 | 44 | 44 | 17.89 | 17.886 |
| 1 | 12 | 56 | 4.88 | 22.764 |
| 2 | 19 | 75 | 7.72 | 30.488 |
| 3 | 25 | 100 | 10.16 | 40.650 |
| 4 | 17 | 117 | 6.91 | 47.561 |
| 5 | 35 | 152 | 14.23 | 61.789 |
| 6 | 35 | 187 | 14.23 | 76.016 |
| 7 | 8 | 195 | 3.25 | 79.268 |
| 8 | 13 | 208 | 5.28 | 84.553 |
| 9 | 19 | 227 | 7.72 | 92.276 |
| 10 | 5 | 232 | 2.03 | 94.309 |
| 11 | 14 | 246 | 5.69 | 100.00 |

The calculator frequency values of second occupational choice of Arts and Science Students with low self efficacy reveals that 17.89% of students have not given their second occupational choice. But how ever 14.23% of Science Arts Students preferred to become Botanist and Physiotherapist, Authors and Charted Accountants. Where as 10.16% of students preferred to opt Architect and collector Profession.

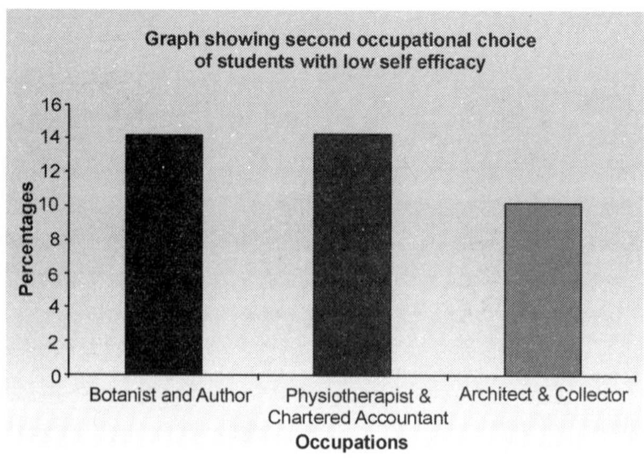

**Table 5.5. Showing First Occupational Choices (Frequencies) of Students with High Self-Efficacy**

| Occupa-tions | Frequ-ency | Cumu-lative-frequency | Percen-tage | Cumulative percentage |
|---|---|---|---|---|
| 1 | 110 | 110 | 28.06 | 28.061 |
| 2 | 139 | 249 | 35.46 | 63.520 |
| 3 | 18 | 267 | 4.59 | 68.112 |
| 4 | 26 | 293 | 6.63 | 74.745 |
| 5 | 9 | 302 | 2.30 | 77.041 |
| 6 | 11 | 313 | 2.81 | 79.847 |
| 7 | 15 | 328 | 3.83 | 83.673 |
| 8 | 12 | 340 | 3.06 | 86.735 |
| 9 | 10 | 350 | 2.55 | 89.286 |
| 10 | 14 | 364 | 3.57 | 92.857 |
| 11 | 28 | 392 | 7.14 | 100.000 |

The calculated frequency values of Arts and Science students with high self-efficacy reveals that 35.46% of science students first occupational choice is Engineering profession and Arts students preference is to become judge. 28.06% of Science students preferred Doctor profession, where as Arts students preferred Lawyer profession. 7.14% of Science and Arts students preferred vocation of their choice. Statistical analysis depicts that the students with high self-efficacy have shown diversified interests and challenging jobs.

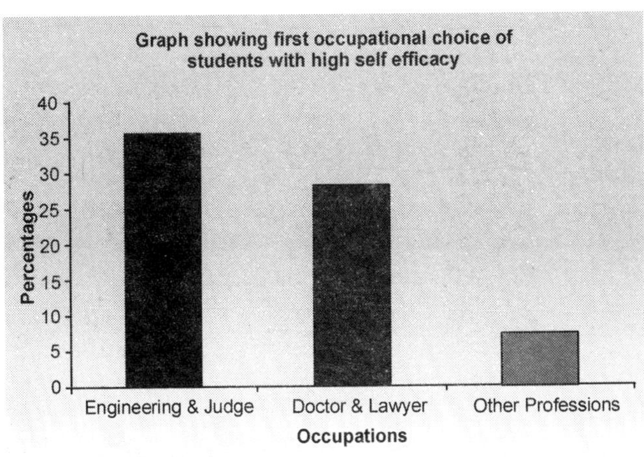

**Table 5.6. Showing Second Occupational Choices (Frequencies) of Students with High Self-efficacy**

| Occupa-tions | Frequ-ency | Cumu-lative-frequency | Percen-tage | Cumulative percentage |
|---|---|---|---|---|
| 0 | 46 | 46 | 11.73 | 11.735 |
| 1 | 21 | 67 | 5.36 | 17.092 |
| 2 | 41 | 108 | 10.46 | 27.551 |
| 3 | 47 | 155 | 11.99 | 39.541 |
| 4 | 31 | 186 | 7.91 | 47.449 |
| 5 | 61 | 247 | 15.56 | 63.010 |
| 6 | 49 | 296 | 12.50 | 75.510 |
| 7 | 22 | 318 | 5.61 | 81.122 |
| 8 | 17 | 335 | 4.34 | 85.459 |
| 9 | 23 | 358 | 5.87 | 91.327 |
| 10 | 18 | 376 | 4.59 | 95.918 |
| 11 | 16 | 392 | 4.08 | 100.00 |

Calculated frequency value reveals that 15.56% of science and arts students with high self-efficacy preferred to become Botanists and Authors, where as 12.50% of Science and Arts students preferred Physiotherapy and Chartered accountant professions. 11.99% Science and Arts students preferred Architect and Collector profession.

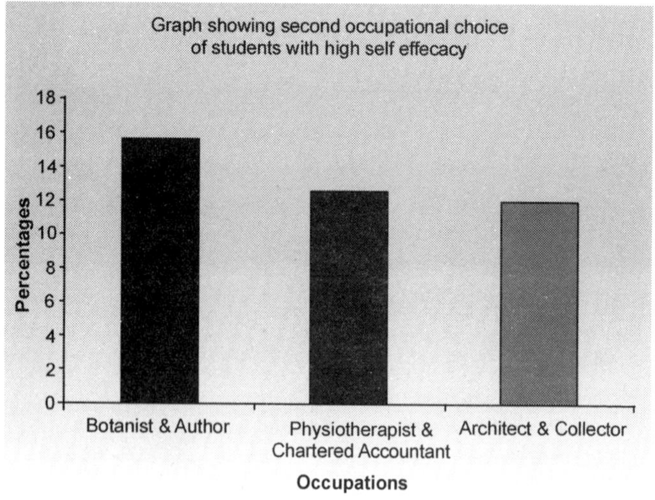

The statistical analysis depict that the students with high self-efficacy have shown broad awareness of vocations and have diversified vocational choice than the students with low self-efficacy. The students with low self-efficacy have stereotype vocational choice with improper knowledge of their abilities, and are over ambitious than the students with high-self-efficacy.

## Hypothesis-3

"There is no significant difference of high - low self-efficacy on 16-personality factors".

Results pertaining to this hypothesis are presented in the table 5.7

**Table 5.7. Showing Mean Standard Deviation and t-Values of Students with Low and High Self-efficacy**

| Factors | Low Self-efficacy High Self-efficacy | | | | |
|---|---|---|---|---|---|
| | Mean Deviation | Stan-dard | Mean deviation | Standard deviation | t-value |
| Factor-A | 5.248 | 1.955 | 5.077 | 1.912 | 1.087@ |
| Factor-B | 7.333 | 2.102 | 7.314 | 2.209 | 0.112@ |
| Factor-C | 1.492 | 1.089 | 1.286 | 1.038 | 2.371* |
| Factor-E | 5.199 | 1.845 | 5.033 | 1.945 | 1.083@ |
| Factor-F | 5.695 | 1.940 | 5.372 | 1.866 | 2.075* |
| Factor-G | 4.695 | 2.006 | 4.684 | 1.901 | 0.072@ |
| Factor-H | 5.537 | 1.929 | 5.730 | 1.964 | 1.222@ |
| Factor-I | 5.919 | 2.039 | 5.745 | 1.955 | 1.065@ |
| Factor-L | 6.366 | 1.847 | 6.584 | 1.859 | 1.450@ |
| Factor-M | 6.561 | 1.886 | 6.536 | 1.964 | 0.162@ |
| Factor-N | 4.622 | 2.022 | 4.349 | 1.840 | 1.714@ |
| Factor-O | 6.431 | 2.008 | 6.283 | 2.287 | 0.857@ |
| Factor-Q1 | 5.870 | 2.085 | 5.584 | 2.080 | 1.686@ |
| Factor-Q2 | 6.293 | 1.851 | 6.885 | 1.683 | 4.074** |
| FactorQ3 | 6.472 | 1.935 | 6.293 | 1.983 | 1.121@ |
| FactorQ4 | 5.915 | 2.063 | 6.071 | 1.930 | 0.958@ |
| Total all factors | 88.691 | 8.610 | 88.911 | 9.315 | 0.304@ |

Low N=246 High N=392

@ not significant

*significant at 0.05 level.

** Significant at 0.01 levels.

**1. Factor-A** the calculated t-value reveals that there is no significant difference of high or low self-efficacy on personality factor-A i.e. Being aloof or being warm and outgoing.

**2. Factor-B** the calculated t-value reveals that there is no significant difference of high or low self-efficacy on being dull or bright.

**3. Factor-C** the calculated t-value reveals that there is significant (2.371*) difference of high or low self-efficacy on emotional (general instability) or mature (egocentric) nature. Higher the self-efficacy higher the emotional stability lower the self-efficacy lower the emotional stability is.

Low score for factor-C depicts emotional immaturity, lack of frustration tolerance, neurotically figured, worrying, easily annoyed, generally dissatisfied, have neurotic symptoms, such as phobia, somatic complaints.

Lower the self-efficacy higher the emotional instability. Higher the self-efficacy lowers the emotional instability.

High scores in factor-c depict emotional maturity, stability, being calm, phlegmatic, realistic, and placid, possess ego strength, and have integrated philosophy of life with high morale.

**4. Factor-E** the calculated t-values reveals that there is no significant difference of high or low self-efficacy on being submissive or dominant nature.

**5. Factor-F** the calculated t-value shows that there is significant (2.075*) difference of high or low self efficacy on being glum, silent (desurgency) or enthusiastic (assurgency).

Low score in factor-F depicts reticent, introspective, communicative, melancholic, anxious, depressed, smug, languid, and slow nature.

High scores depict cheerful, talkative, frank, expressive, quick, alert, imperturbable, chosen as an elected leader. Lower the self-efficacy glum and silent nature exist. Higher the self-efficacy enthusiastic nature exists.

**6. Factor–G** the calculated t-value reveals that there is no significant difference of high or low self-efficacy on factor-G i.e. being casual or conscientious.

**7. Factor-H** the calculated t-value revels that there is no significant difference of high or low self-efficacy on factor-H i.e. being timid or adventurous.

**8. Factor-I** the calculated t-value reveals that there is no significant difference of high or low self-efficacy on factor-I. Being tough or sensitive.

**9. Factor-L** the calculated t-value reveals that there is no significant difference of high or low self-efficacy on factor-L i.e. being trustful or being suspecting.

**10. Factor-M** the calculated t-value reveals that there is no significant difference of high or low self-efficacy on factor-M i.e. being conventional or being eccentric.

**11. Factor-N** the calculated t-value reveals that there is no difference of high or low self-efficacy on personality factor-N i.e. being simple or sophisticated.

**12. Factor-O** the calculated t-value reveals that there is no significant difference of high or low self-efficacy on personality factor-O i.e. being confident or insecure.

**13. Factor-Q1** the calculated t-value reveals that there is significant (4.074**) difference of high or low self-efficacy on personality factor-Q1 i.e. being conservative or being experimenting.

Low scores in personality factor-Q1 indicates individual is cautious, moderate, opposed to any change, inclined to go along with tradition, not interested in analytical thought.

High scores in personality factor-Q1 indicte that the individual is interested in intellectual matters and fundamental issues, well informed, less inclined to moralise, more inclined to experimentation, more tolerant of inconvenience.

Lower the self-efficacy conservative the individual is and higher the self-efficacy more experimenting the individual is. It means high self-efficacy enhances beliefs on ones abilities, foresight, and understanding.

**14. Factor-Q2** the calculated t-value reveals that there is significant difference of high or low self-efficacy on personality factorQ2 i.e. being dependent or being self-sufficient.

**15. Factor-Q3** the calculated t-value reveals that there is no significant difference of high or low self-efficacy on personality factor-Q3 i.e. being uncontrolled or being self-controlled.

**16. Factor-Q4** the calculated t-value reveals that there is no significant difference of high or low self-efficacy on personality factor-Q4 i.e. being stable or being tense.

**16-Personality Factors** the calculated t-value reveal that there is no significant difference of high or low self-efficacy on 16-personality factors.

Hence the hypothesis "there is no significant difference of high-low self-efficacy on 16-personality factors" gets accepted.

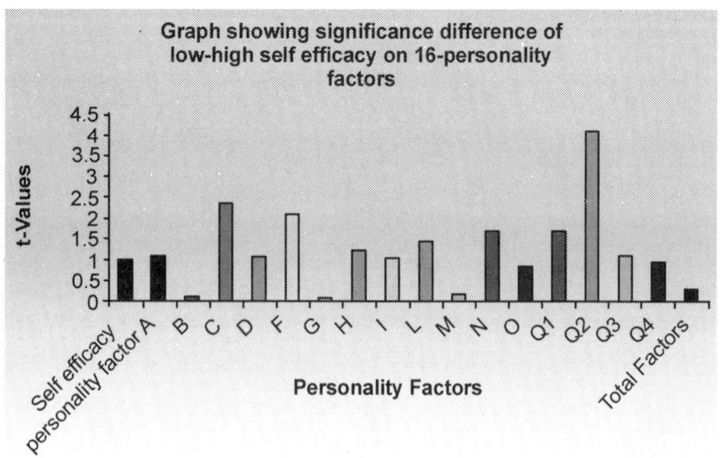


The researcher was interested to find out first and second occupational choice of Arts and Science Students with low and high intelligence. Occupation preferences as shown in the following tables. Only three preferences with high frequency were considered and remained preferences were omitted.

**Table 5.8. Showing First Occupational Preference as Students with Low Intelligance**

| Occupa-tions | Frequ-ency | Cumu-lative-frequency | Percen-tage | Cumulative percentage |
|---|---|---|---|---|
| 1 | 94 | 94 | 36.02 | 36.015 |
| 2 | 57 | 57 | 21.84 | 57.854 |
| 3 | 9 | 160 | 3.45 | 61.303 |
| 4 | 19 | 179 | 7.28 | 68.582 |
| 5 | 8 | 187 | 3.07 | 71.648 |
| 6 | 8 | 195 | 3.07 | 74.713 |
| 7 | 11 | 206 | 4.21 | 78.927 |
| 8 | 9 | 215 | 3.45 | 82.375 |
| 9 | 11 | 226 | 4.21 | 86.590 |
| 10 | 10 | 236 | 3.83 | 90.421 |
| 11 | 25 | 261 | 9.58 | 100.000 |

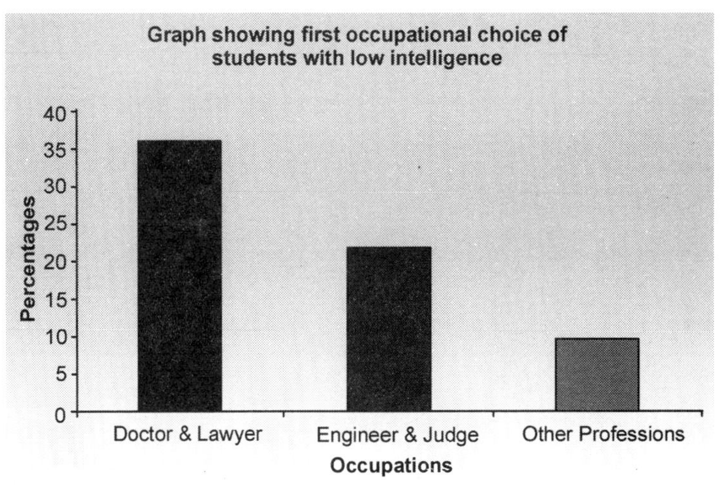

The calculated frequency values of first occupational choice reveal that Science and Arts students with low intelligence preferred Doctor and Lawyer (36.02%) profession, Engineering and Judge profession (21.87%) other profession (9.58%) of their choice.

**Table 5.9. Showing Second Occupational Choice of Students with Low Intelligence**

| Occupa-tions | Frequ-ency | Cumu-lative-frequency | Percen-tage | Cumulative percentage |
|---|---|---|---|---|
| 0 | 47 | 47 | 18.01 | 18.008 |
| 1 | 19 | 66 | 7.28 | 25.287 |
| 2 | 27 | 93 | 10.34 | 35.632 |
| 3 | 16 | 109 | 6.13 | 41.762 |
| 4 | 21 | 130 | 8.05 | 49.808 |
| 5 | 41 | 171 | 15.71 | 65.517 |
| 6 | 39 | 210 | 14.94 | 80.460 |
| 7 | 8 | 218 | 3.07 | 83.525 |
| 8 | 11 | 229 | 4.21 | 87.739 |
| 9 | 15 | 244 | 5.75 | 93.487 |
| 10 | 10 | 254 | 3.83 | 97.318 |
| 11 | 7 | 261 | 2.68 | 100.000 |

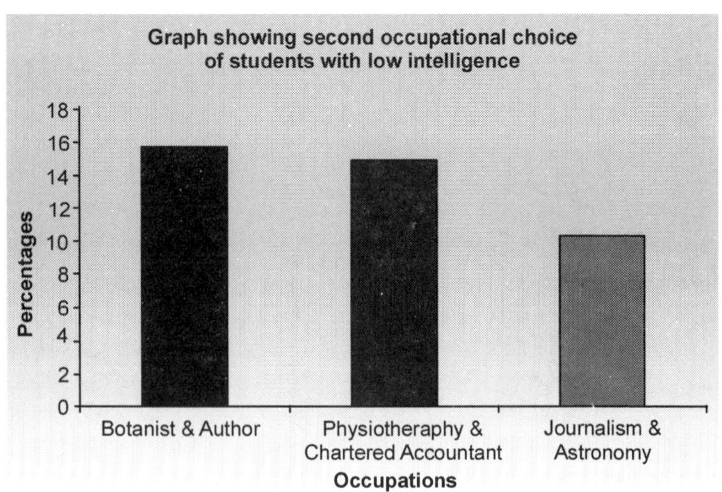

Calculated frequency value reveals that 18.01% of Arts and Science Students have not listed their second occupational choice. 15.71% of Arts and Science Students preferred Botanist and Author profession. 14.94% students preferred Physiotherapy and Chartered accountant. 10.34% students preferred Journalism and Astronomy.

**Table 5.10. Showing First Occupational Preference of Students with High Intelligence**

| Occupations | Frequency | Cumulative-frequency | Percentage | Cumulative percentage |
|---|---|---|---|---|
| 1 | 99 | 99 | 26.68 | 26.685 |
| 2 | 154 | 253 | 41.51 | 68.194 |
| 3 | 14 | 267 | 3.77 | 71.968 |
| 4 | 16 | 283 | 4.31 | 76.280 |
| 5 | 8 | 291 | 2.16 | 78.437 |
| 6 | 10 | 301 | 2.70 | 81.132 |
| 7 | 13 | 314 | 3.50 | 84.636 |
| 8 | 11 | 325 | 2.96 | 87.601 |
| 9 | 5 | 330 | 1.35 | 88.949 |
| 10 | 11 | 341 | 2.96 | 91.914 |
| 11 | 30 | 371 | 8.09 | 100.000 |

The calculated frequency value reveal that the first occupational choice of science and arts students with high intelligence is engineer, judge (41.51%) doctor and lawyer (26.68%), vocation of their choice (8.01%).

That means students with high intelligence are opting for high jobs with self awareness.

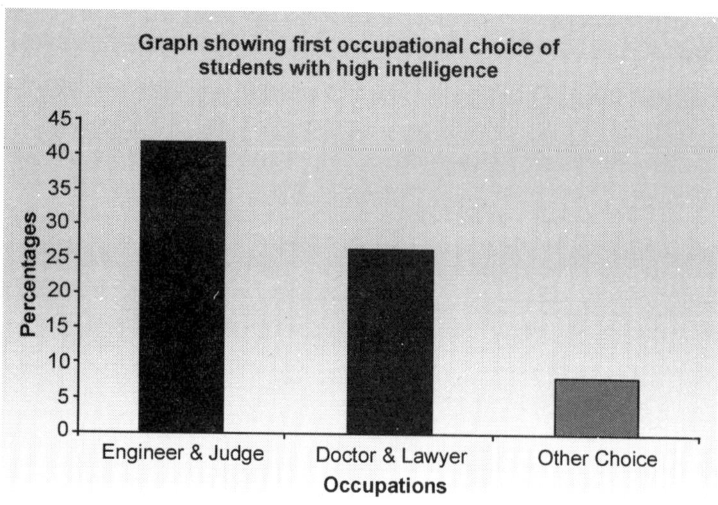


**Table 5.11. Showing Second Occupational Choice of Students with High Intelligence**

| Occupations | Frequency | Cumulative-frequency | Percentage | Cumulative percentage |
|---|---|---|---|---|
| 0 | 35 | 35 | 9.43 | 9.434 |
| 1 | 12 | 47 | 3.23 | 12.668 |
| 2 | 40 | 87 | 10.78 | 23.450 |
| 3 | 59 | 146 | 15.90 | 39.353 |
| 4 | 22 | 168 | 5.93 | 45.283 |
| 5 | 55 | 223 | 14.82 | 60.108 |
| 6 | 46 | 269 | 12.40 | 72.507 |
| 7 | 20 | 289 | 5.39 | 77.898 |
| 8 | 19 | 308 | 5.12 | 83.019 |
| 9 | 25 | 333 | 6.74 | 89.757 |
| 10 | 18 | 351 | 4.85 | 94.609 |
| 11 | 20 | 371 | 5.39 | 100.000 |

The calculated frequency value reveals that the second occupational choice of students with high intelligence is Architect, Collector 15.90%), Botanist, Author (14.82%), Physiotherapist, Chartered accountant (12.40%).

The results reveal that the students with high intelligence have shown diversified interests in occupational choice with administrative interest.

However there is no significant relation between the intelligence and occupational preferences of Science and Arts students. Both of them have stereotype occupational choice irrespective of their intelligence and self efficacy.

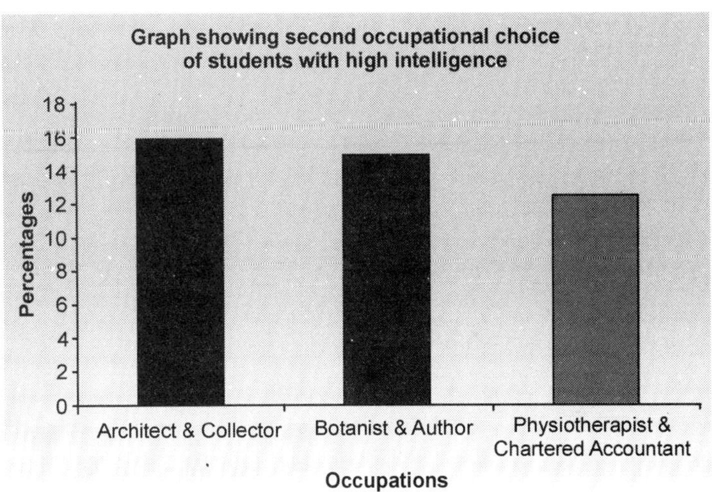


**Hypothesis-4**

"There is no significant difference of High or Low intelligence on personality factors".

Results pertaining to this hypothesis are presented in the table 5.12

**Table 5.12. Showing Mean Standard Deviation t-values of 16-personality Factors with Low and High Intelligence**

| Factors | Low Intelli-gence n=261 | | High Intelli-gence n=371 | | t-value |
|---|---|---|---|---|---|
| | Mean | Standard deviation | Mean | Standard deviation | |
| Facor-A | 5.406 | 1.972 | 5.062 | 1.880 | 2.202* |
| Facor-B | 7.659 | 2.123 | 6.911 | 2.172 | 4.319** |
| Facor-C | 1.326 | 1.031 | 1.404 | 1.083 | 0.925@ |
| Facor-E | 5.111 | 1.879 | 5.208 | 2.010 | 0.617@ |
| Facor-F | 5.552 | 1.896 | 5.377 | 1.847 | 1.150@ |
| Facor-G | 4.916 | 1.869 | 4.507 | 1.931 | 2.671** |
| Facor-H | 5.594 | 1.858 | 5.604 | 1.874 | 0.066@ |
| Facor-I | 5.862 | 2.159 | 6.013 | 1.965 | 0.900@ |
| Facor-L | 6.536 | 1.839 | 6.582 | 1.903 | 0.304@ |
| Facor-M | 6.632 | 1.913 | 6.482 | 1.973 | 0.956@ |
| Facor-N | 4.567 | 1.948 | 4.340 | 1.990 | 1.432@ |
| Facor-O | 6.517 | 2.161 | 6.251 | 2.234 | 1.506@ |
| Facor-Q1 | 5.682 | 2.057 | 5.836 | 2.176 | 0.902@ |
| Facor-Q2 | 6.590 | 1.655 | 6.741 | 1.789 | 1.093@ |
| Facor-Q3 | 6.149 | 1.909 | 6.491 | 1.929 | 2.202* |
| Facor-Q4 | 6.015 | 1.881 | 5.938 | 2.135 | 0.481@ |
| Total Facors | 88.659 | 9.507 | 88.903 | 7.956 | 0.339@ |

@not significant
*correlation is significant at the 0.05 level.
**correlation Is significant at the 0.01 level

**1. Factor-A** the calculated t-value reveals that there is significant (2.202*significant at 0.05 level) difference of high or low intelligence on personality factor –A. That means higher the intelligence more warm and outgoing the individual is and lower the intelligence aloof stiff and cool the individual is. It means the children with high intelligence are more extroverts, warm and outgoing good natured, easy going, ready to cooperate, attentive to people, soft hearted, kind, trustworthy, adaptable where as the children with low intelligence are introverts shy, withdrawn, aloof, cool and stiff in personality traits.

**2. Factor-B** the calculated t-value reveals that there is significant (4.319** significant at 0.01 level) difference of high or low intelligence on personality factor-B i.e. being dull or bright.

It means that higher the intelligence bright and intelligent the individual is and lower the intelligence dull sluggish, bookish, with little taste for high form of knowledge.

**3. Factor-C** the calculated t-value reveals that there is no significant difference of high or low intelligence on personality factor-C i.e. being emotional or being mature.

**4. Factor-E** the calculated t-value reveals that there is no significant difference of high or low intelligence on personality factor- E i.e. being submissive or dominant.

**5. Factor-F** the calculated t-value reveals that there is no significant difference of high or low intelligence on personality factor-F i.e. being glum or enthusiastic.

**6. Factor-G** the calculated t-value reveals that there is significant difference of high or low intelligence on personality factor-G i.e. being casual or conscientious.

Low score indicates that the individual is fickle minded, undependable, irresolute, unsteady, quitting, sometimes demanding, impatience, indolent, destructive and lack internal standards.

Where as high score indicates that individual is strong, persevering, responsible, determined, consistent, planful, energetic, and cautious, well organised, high regard for moral standards, and prefers efficient companions. It means that higher the intelligence more conscientious the individual is and lower the intelligence casual the individual is.

**7. Factor-H** the calculated t-value reveals that there is no significant difference of high or low intelligence on personality factor-I i.e. being timid or adventurous.

**8. Factor-I** the calculated t-value reveals that there is significant difference of high or low intelligence on personality factor-I i.e. Being tough or sensitive.

**9. Factor-L** the calculated t-value reveals that there is no significant difference of high or low intelligence on personality factor-L i.e. .being trustful or suspecting.

**10. Factor-M** the calculated t-value reveals that there is no significant difference of high or low intelligence on personality factor- M i.e. being conventional or eccentric.

**11. Factor-N** the calculated t-value reveals that there is no significant difference of high or low intelligence on personality factor-N i.e. being simple or sophisticated.

**12. Factor-O** the calculated t-value reveals that there is no significant difference of high or low intelligence on personality factor-O i.e. being confident or being insecure.

**13. Factor-Q1** the calculated t-value reveals that there is no significant difference of high or low intelligence on personality factor-Q1.i.e. Being conservative or experimenting.

**14. Factor-Q2** the calculated t-value reveals that there is no significant difference of high or low intelligence on personality factor-Q2.i.e being dependent or self-sufficient.

**15. Factor-Q3** the calculated t-value reveals that there is significant difference of high or low (2.202* significant at 0.05 level) intelligence on personality factor-Q3 i.e. being uncontrolled or being controlled.

High values in personality factorQ3 indicates that the individual has strong control of emotions, general behaviour, considerate, careful, self-respect, sometimes obstinate, effective leader.

Low score in personality factor-Q3 indicate that the individual has no will control no character stability, not too considerate, careful, and conscientious.

**16. Factor-Q4** the calculated t-value reveals that there is no significant difference of high or low intelligence on personality factor-Q4.i.e.being stable or tense.

## TOTAL ALL 16- PERSONALITY FACTORS

The calculated t-value reveals that there is no significant difference of high or low intelligence on total 16-personality factors.

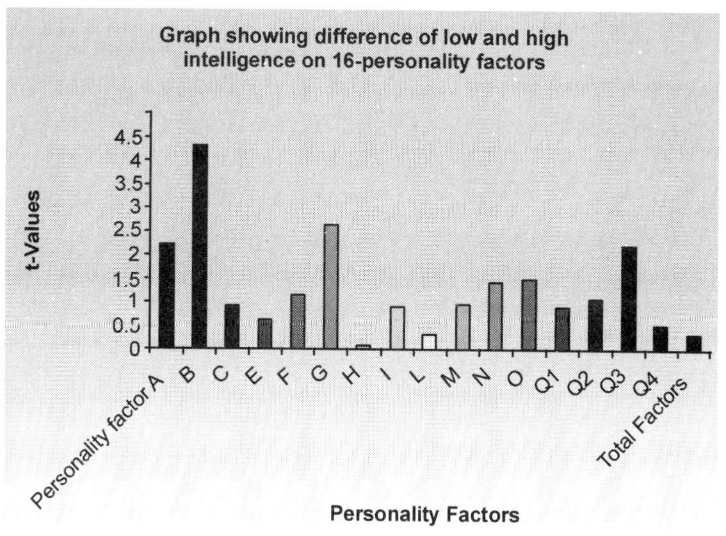


## MULTIPLE REGRESSION ANALYSIS

The main focus of the present study is to assess the contribution of the independent variables, singly and in combination, to the variance to self-efficacy, intelligence, 16-personality factors and first and second occupational choice. All methods of analysis seek to identify and quantify variance shared by variables. Multiple regressions seek to identify and estimate the magnitude and statically significance of the variance of the dependent variable. The effort is directed toward explaining a single phenomenon, which is complex and has various facets, multiple regressions in close to the theoretical and inferential preoccupations and methods of scientific behavioural research (Cohen, 1968).

Although multiple regression analyses of variance are inter-changeable in the case of categorical independent variables, multiple regression analysis is superior or the only appropriate method of analysis in the following cases.

1. When the independent variable is continuous, that is experimental treatments with varying degrees of the same variable.
2. When the independent variables are both continuous and categorical.
3. When frequencies in a factorial design are unequal and disproportionate, and when studying trends in data.

Since the variables employed in the present investigation fit into the conditions described above, multiple regression analysis appeared to be the most appropriate method of analysis. Multiple regression analysis is often the best method of analysis even for non-experimental data (pedhazur, 1973).

It is suited to almost any non-experimental research in which there are several independent variables and one or two dependent variable. No matter what the scales of measurement are or what the kind of variable is. Useful analysis can be done and interpretations made by using multiple regression analysis (kerlinger andpedhazur, 1973).

The final strength of multiple regression analysis is its rich yield of various statistics to be used in the interpretation. The measure of overall relation between the independent variable and the dependent variables,R2, (which is an estimate of the proportion of variance accounted for, by all the variables or any subset of them), and 'F' tests of the statistical significance of different R2's are routinely calculated apart from partial correlation coefficients and standard error. Multiple regression analysis cannot be stated as lacking in shortcomings. The reliability of the results of multiple regression analysis is a problem of the method. In any case, the larger the sample size the more precise the statistical analysis.

In the present study step-wise regression analysis was used to test the hypothesis that there is no significant effect of demographical factors on self-efficacy, intelligence, personality and occupational choice.

Step-wise regression is an important type of multiple regression analysis in which the independent variables were selectively entered in the regression analysis in order to obtain their contribution. The order of entry was determined by the highest amount of contribution made by a variable followed the others. Partial correlations indicate the relation between the variables when other variables or sources of influence on the dependent variable are controlled or held constant. i.e. unwanted influence is removed from both variables of the correlation. F- Ratio indicates the significance of the partial correlations.

## Category-I

Firstly, the analysis was made for dependent variable self-efficacy and various demographical factors such as gender, nativity, and parent's educational qualifications, type of the college and group or subject.

Values have not entered instep wise multiple analysis as there is no statistically significant value on self-efficacy.

Hence the hypotheses that

## Hypothesis-5

"There is no significant effect of Gender on self-efficacy"

## Hypothesis-6

"There is no significant effect of nativity on self-efficacy".

## Hypothesis-7

"There is no significant effect of educational qualifications of parents on self-efficacy".

### Hypothesis-8

"There is no significant effect of type of the college on self-efficacy".

### Hypothesis-9

There is no significant effect of group (subject) on self-efficacy". Gets disapproved.

### Category-II

The Second analysis was made for the dependent variable Intelligence and five demographical factors i.e. gender, nativity, parent's educational qualifications type of the college and group or subject are presented in the table 5.13.

### Hypothesis-10

"There is no significant effect of Gender, on intelligence".

### Hypothesis-11

"There is no significant effect of nativity on intelligence."

### Hypothesis-12

"There is no significant effect of educational qualifications of parents on intelligence."

### Hypothesis-13

"There is no significant effect of type of the college on intelligence."

### Hypothesis-14

"There is no significant effect of group (subject) on intelligence."

Out of five independent variables, the variable that has the highest zero order correlation with intelligence was entered first (such being the usual practice) in the regression equation. The R2 for independent variable Group 0.11795 is significant at .0l level and F-value 120.74.

**Table 5.13. Showing Regression Analysis for Demographical Factors and Intelligence (N=900)**

| S. No. | Variable | R | R2 | F-value To enter |
|---|---|---|---|---|
| 1 | Group | 0.3434 | 0.11795 | 120.74* |
| 2. | Parental educational qualifications | 0.3578 | 0.12799 | 66.19** |

** Significant at .01 level

The independent variable parental educational qualification was entered in the second step, since it has the highest partial correlation and consequently higher "F"-value to enter 66.1975 which is significant at .01 levels. The addition of this variable has increased the R2 by .01004 that is it additionally accounted for 1% of the variance to intelligence. The combination of two variables (R2 .12799) explains 12% of the variance to intelligence.

The other three independent variables have not entered as there is no statistically significant value.

Hence the hypothesis

1. "There is no significant effect of gender on intelligence" gets approved.
2. "There is no significant effect of nativity on intelligence gets approved.

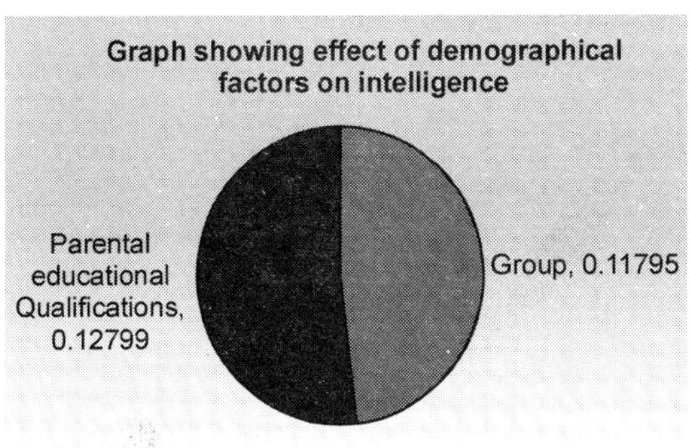

3. "There is no significant effect of parental educational qualifications on intelligence." gets rejected.
4. There is no significant effect of type of the college on intelligence" gets accepted.
5. "There is no significant effect of group (subject) on intelligence" gets rejected.

**Category-III**

Third analysis was made for five demographical factors Gender, nativity, parents' educational qualifications, type of the college and group (subject) and first occupational choice. Values are presented in the table-5.14.

**Hypothesis-15**

"There is no significant effect of gender on first occupational choice".

**Hypothesis-16**

"There is no significant effect of nativity on first occupational choice".

**Hypothesis-17**

"There is no significant effect of parent's educational qualifications on first occupational choice.

**Hypothesis-18**

"There is no significant effect of type of the college on first occupational choice."

**Hypothesis-19**

"There is no significant effect of Group (Subject) on first occupational choice."

Among five independent variables the variable 'group' was entered first as it has highest zero order correlation with first occupational choice in the regression equation. The R2 for Group is 0.08631 and F-value (85.29672) is significant at 0.01 level. And its contribution is 8.63%to occupational choice. As increase in R2 due to this variable is significant it was retained in the equation.

**Table 5.14. Showing Regression Analyses for Demographical Factor and First Occupational Choice**

| S. No. | Variable | R | R2 | F-value To enter |
|---|---|---|---|---|
| 1. | Group | 0.2938 | 0.08631 | 85.29** |
| 2 | Type of the college | 0.3080 | 0.09488 | 47.27** |

**significant at .01 level

The variable 'type of the college' was entered in the second place since it has the highest partial correlation and consequently higher "F" value to enter 47.27639 which is significant at 0.01 level. The addition of this variable 'type of the college' has increased the R2 by .0857, and it additionally accounted for 8.5 %of the variance to occupational choice. The combination of the two variables (R2 .09488) explains 9% of the variance to occupational choice.

The statistical analysis reveals that there is the effect of 'group' and 'type of the college' on the occupational choice of students. The other three variables were not entered as there is no statistically significant value of them on occupational choice. Hence the

1. Hypothesis that "there is no significant effect of gender on first occupational choice." Gets accepted.
2. Hypothesis that "there is no significant effect of nativity on first occupational choice gets accepted.
3. Hypothesis that "there is no significant effect of educational qualifications of parents on first occupational choice" gets accepted.
4. Hypothesis that "there is no significant effect of type of the college on first occupational choice "gets disproved.

5. Hypothesis that "there is no significant effect of group (subject) on first occupational choice" gets rejected.

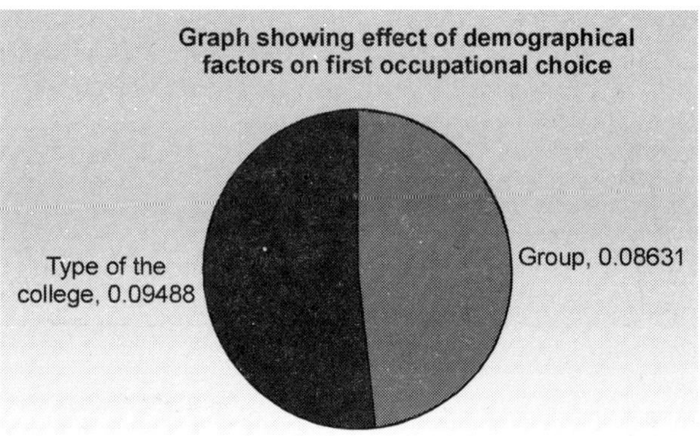


## Category-IV

Fourth analysis was made for five demographical factors gender, nativity, parents' educational qualifications, type of the college, and group (subject) and second occupational choice and values were presented in the table 5.15.

### Hypothesis-20

"There is no significant effect of gender on second occupational choice".

### Hypothesis-21

"There is no significant effect of nativity on second occupational choice".

### Hypothesis-22

"There is no significant effect of parent's educational qualifications on second occupational choice.

### Hypothesis-23

"There is no significant effect of type of the college on second occupational choice."

## Hypothesis-24

"There is no significant effect of group (subject) on second occupational choice."

**Table 5.15. Showing Regression Analysis for Demographical Factors and Second Occupational Choice**

| S. No. | Variable | R | R2 | F-value To enter |
|---|---|---|---|---|
| 1. | Group | 0.2591 | 0.06713 | 64.98** |

**significant at .01 level

Among five demographical factors only one variable i.e. group has the highest zero order correlation with second occupational choice was entered in the regression equation. The R2 for 'group' is 0.06713 is significant at 0.05 level and its contribution is 25%, and F-value is 64.98.

Among five demographical factors only 'group' affect's the second occupational choice of the students. Hence the hypothesis.

1. "There is no effect of gender on second occupational choice" gets approved.
2. "There is no significant effect of nativity on second occupational choice." Gets approved.
3. "There is no significant effect of educational qualifications of parents on second occupational choice" gets accepted.
4. "There is no significant effect of type of the college on second occupational choice." Gets accepted.
5. "There is no significant effect of group (subject) On second occupational choice." Gets disapproved.

## Category-V

Fifth analysis was made to observe the effect of five demographical factors i.e. gender, nativity, educational qualifications of parents, type of the college, and group on 16-personality factors.

## Hypothesis-25

"There is no significant effect of demographical factors on personality factors-A".

Results pertaining to this hypothesis are presented in the table 5.16.

**Table 5.16. Table showing Step-wise Regression Analysis for Personality Factor-A and Demographical Factors**

| S. No. | Variable | R | R2 | F-value To enter |
|---|---|---|---|---|
| 1. | Group | 0.0808 | 0.00652 | 5.929114** |
| 2. | Type of the college | 0.1052 | 0.01106 | 5.044393** |
| 3. | Educational qualifications of parents | 0.1238 | 0.01533 | 4.676584* |

*significant at .05 level
**significant at .01 level.

Out of the five independent variables, the variable that has highest zero order correlation with factor – A was entered first (such being the usual practice) in the regression equation. The R2 for group is .00652 is significant at 0.01 level and its contribution is .6% to personality factor –A as the increase in R2 due to this variable is significant it was retained in the equation F-value is 5.92.

The variable 'type of the college' was entered in the second step, since it has the highest partial correlation and consequently higher "F" to enter 5.04393 which is significant at 0.01 levels. The addition of this variable 'type of the college' has increased the R2 by 0.00454 that is it additionally accounted for .4% of the variance to personality factor-A. The combination of the two variables (R2.01106) explains 11% of the variance.

In the third step, educational qualifications of parents were entered as that has the next highest "F" value to enter 4.6765. This variable has additionally contributed about 1% of the variance to factor –A, as is shown by the increase in

R2.0153. the combination of the three variables group, type of the college , and educational qualifications of the parents accounted for (R2.01533) 1% of the variance to factor-A.

The other variables were not entered in the step wise solution as they have no significant value.

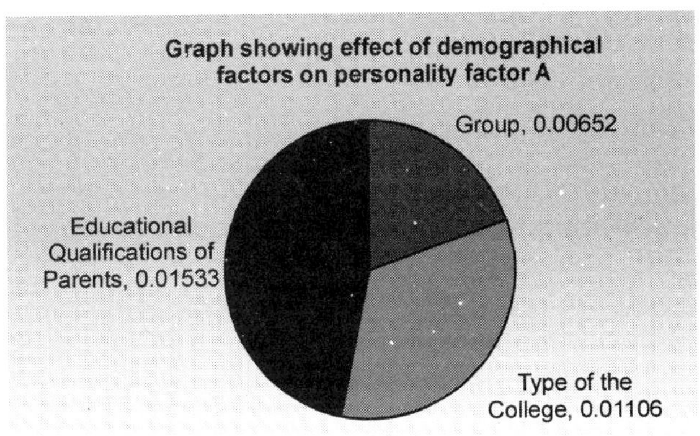


## Hypothesis-26

"There is no significant effect of demographical factors on personality factor-B"

Results pertaining to this hypothesis are presented in the table 5.17.

**Table 5.17. Showing Step-wise Regression Analysis for Personality Factor-B and Demographical Factors**

| S. No. | Variable | R | R2 | F-value To enter |
|---|---|---|---|---|
| 1. | Nativity | 0.1024 | 0.01049 | 9.57** |

**significant at .01 level.

Out of the five independent variables the variable that has highest zero order correlation with personality factor-B was entered first in the regression equation. The R2 for nativity is 0.01049.is significant at 0.01 levels and its contribution is 1% to factor-B as the increase in R2 due to this variable is significant it was retained in the equation F-value is 9.57

The other variables have not entered in step wise regression hence they were not recorded.

Hence the hypothesis that "there is no effect of demographical factors on personality factor-B gets disproved.

## Hypothesis-27

"There is no significant effect of demographical on personality factor-C"

Results pertaining to this hypothesis are presented in the table.5.18.

**Table 5.18. Showing Step-wise Regression Analysis of Personality Factor-C and Demographical Factors**

| S. No. | Variable | R | R2 | F-value To enter |
|---|---|---|---|---|
| 1. | Gender | 0.0786 | 0.00618 | 5.61** |

**Significant at .01 level

Out of five independent variables the variable 'gender'. Has highest zero order correlation. The R2 for gender is .00618 is significant at .01` level and its contribution is 6% to factor-C as the increase in R2 due to this variable is significant it was retained in the equation F-value 5.61.

The other variables have not entered in step wise regression as the values were insignificant.

Hence the hypothesis that "there is no significant effect of demographical factors on personality factor-C gets disproved."

## Hypothesis-28

"There is no significant effect of demographical factors on personality factor-E".

Results pertaining to this hypothesis re presented in the table5.19.

**Table 5.19. Showing Step-wise Regressional Analysis of Personality Factor-E and Demographical Factors**

| S. No. | Variable | R | R2 | F-value To enter |
|---|---|---|---|---|
| 1. | Parents education | 0.0609 | 0.00371 | 3.35* |
| 2. | Nativity | 0.0899 | 0.00808 | 3.67* |

*Significant at .05 level

Out of five independent variables the variable 'parents education' that has highest zero order correlation with factor-E was entered first in the regression equation. The R2 for parent's educational qualification is .00371 is significant at.05 level and its contribution is 3% to factor-E. As the increase in R2 due to this variable is significant it was retained in the equation F-value is 3.35

The variable nativity was entered in the second step, since it has the highest partial correlation and consequently higher "F' to enter .3.671.which is significant at 0.05 level. The addition of this variable has increased the R2 by.00437. That is it additionally accounted for 4% of the variance to factor-E. The combination of the two variables (R2.00808) explains 8% of the variance to factor-E.

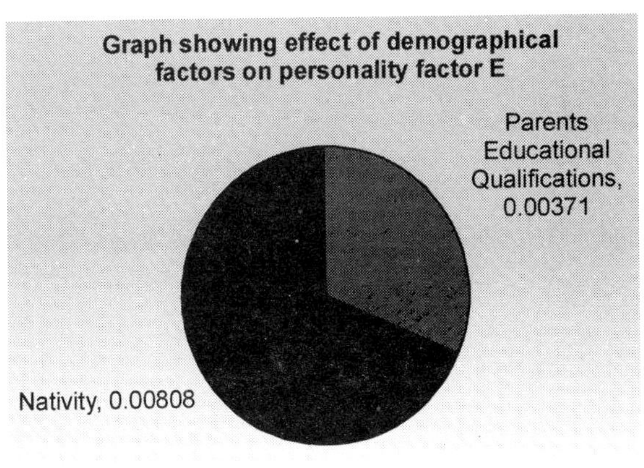

## Hypothesis-29

"There is no significant effect of demographical factors on personality factor-F."

Results pertaining to this hypothesis are presented in the table 5.20.

**Table 5.20. Table Showing Step-wise Regression Analysis for Personality Factor-F and Demographical Factors**

| S. No. | Variable | R | R2 | F-value To enter |
|---|---|---|---|---|
| 1. | Gender | 0.1065 | 0.01134 | 10.35** |
| 2. | Group | 0.1260 | 0.01587 | 7.27** |

**Significant at0.01 level

Out of five independent variables the variable 'gender' was entered first in the regression as the R2 for gender is .01134 is significant at .01 levels and its contribution is 11% to factor-F. As the increase in R2 due to this variable is significant it was retained in the equation F-value is 10.35.

The variable 'group' was entered in the second step, since it has the highest partial correlation and consequently higher "F" to enter 7.27. Which is significant at .01 levels the additional of this variable has increased the R2 by .00453 that is it additionally accounted for 4% of the variance to factor-F. The combination of the two variables (R2.01587) explains 1% of the variance to factor-F.

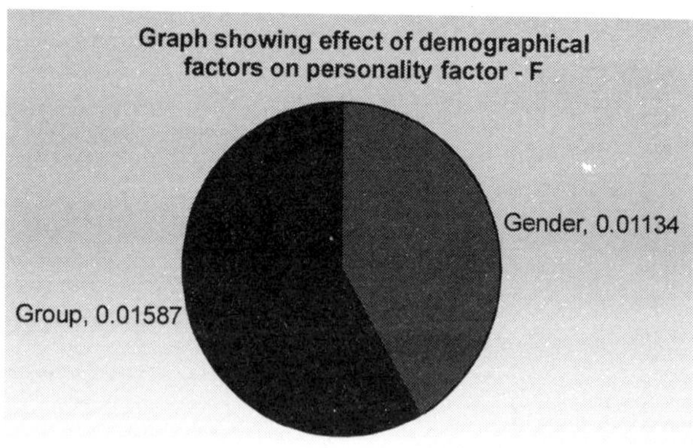

The other variables were not entered in step wise regression as their values were insignificant.

## Hypothesis-30

"There is no significant effect of demographical factors on personality factor-G."

Results pertaining to this hypothesis are presented in the table 5.21.

**Table 5.21. Table Showing Step-wise Regression of Personality Factor-G and Demographical Factors**

| S. No. | Variable | R | R2 | F-value To enter |
|---|---|---|---|---|
| 1. | Type ofcollege | 0.1058 | 0.01120 | 10.22** |
| 2. | Gender | 0.1290 | 0.01664 | 7.63** |
| 3. | Parent'seducation | 0.1434 | 0.02056 | 6.30** |

**significant at 0.01 level.

Out of five independent variables the variable 'type of the college' was entered first in step wise regression as the R2 for type of the college .01120 is significant at .01 levels and its contribution is 1%to factor-G. As the increase R2 due to this variable is significant, it was retained in the equation F-value is 10.22.

The variable 'gender' was entered in the second step, since it has the highest partial correlation and consequently higher "F" to enter 6.306006 which is significant at .01 levels. The Addition of this variable has increased the R2 by .00544, that is, it additionally accounted for 5% of the variance to factor-G. The combination of the two variables (R2 .01664) explains 1% of the variance to factor-G.

In the third, step, 'parents education qualifications' were entered as that has the next highest "F" to enter 6.306006. This variable has additionally contributed about .2% of the variance to factor-G as it shown by the increase in R2.02056. The combination of the three variables accounted for .2% of the variance to factor-G.

The other variables were not entered in step wise regression as their values were insignificant.

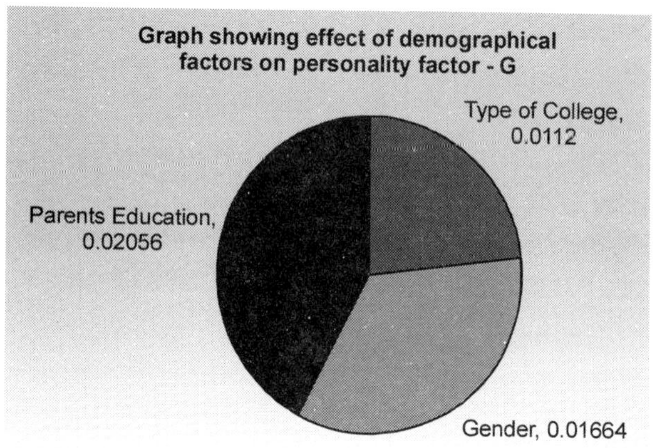


## Hypothesis-31

"There is no significant effect of demographical factors on personality factor-H"

## Factor-H

Five independent variables gender, nativity, parents educational qualifications, type of the college , group have not entered in step wise regression for personality factor-H as their values were insignificant.

Hence the hypothesis that there is no significant effect of demographical on personality factor –H "gets accepted.

## Hypothesis-32

"There is no significant effect of demographical factors on personality factor-I"

## Factor-I

Five independent variable gender, nativity, parents educational qualifications, type of the college and group have not entered in step-wise regression for personality factor-I as their values were insignificant.

Hence the hypothesis that "there is no significant effect of demographical factors on personality factor-I "gets accepted.

## Hypothesis-33

There is no significant effect of demographic factors on personality factor –L."

## Factor-L

Five independent variables gender, nativity, parents educational qualifications, type of the college, and group have not entered in step wise regression for personality factor-L as their values were insignificant.

Hence the hypothesis that there is no significant effect of demographical on personality factor-L gets accepted.

## Hypothesis-34

"There is no significant effect of demographical factors on personality factor-M".

Results pertaining to this hypothesis are presented in the table 5.22.

**Table 5.22. Showing Step-wise Regression Analysis for Personality Factor-M and Demographical Factors**

| S. No. | Variable | R | R2 | F-value To enter |
|---|---|---|---|---|
| 1. | Gender | 0.0913 | 0.00833 | 7.58** |

**Significant at .01 level.

Out of five independent variables the variable 'gender' has entered first in step wise regression equation as the R2 for gender is0.00833 it is significant at .01 levels and its contribution is .8% to factor-M. As the increase in R2 due to this variable is significant it was retained in the equation F-value is 7.58.

The other variables have not entered in step wise regression equation as their values were insignificant.

Hence the hypothesis that "there is no significant effect of demographical on personality factor-M" gets disproved.

### Hypothesis-35

"There is no significant effect of demographical factors on personality factors-N"

Results pertaining to this hypothesis are presented in the table5.23.

**Table 5.23. Showing Step-wise Regression for Personality Factor-N and Demographical Factors**

| S. No. | Variable | R | R2 | F-value To enter |
|---|---|---|---|---|
| 1. | Gender | 0.1668 | 0.02783 | 25.85** |

**significant at .01 level

Out of five independent variables the variable 'gender' was entered first in the step wise regression the R2 for gender is 0.2783. It is significant at. 01 levels and its contribution is 27% to factor-N as the increase in R2 due to this variable is significant; it was retained in the equation F-value is 25.85.

The other four variables have not entered in step wise regression as their values were not significant.

Hence the hypothesis that "there is no significant effect of demographical factors on personality factor-N" gets rejected.

### Hypothesis-36

"There is no significant effect of demographical factors on personality factor-O"

### Factor-O

Five independent variables have not entered in step wise regression as their values were not significant.

Hence the hypothesis that "there is no significant effect of demographical on personality factor-O" gets accepted.

## Hypothesis-37

"There is no significant effect of demographical factors on personality factor-Q1".

Results pertaining to this hypothesis are presented in the table 5.24.

**Table 5.24. Showing Step-wise Regression Analysis for Personality Factor-Q1 and Demographical Factors**

| S. No. | Variable | R | R2 | F-value To enter |
|---|---|---|---|---|
| 1 | Gender | 0.2889 | 0.08348 | 82.25** |
| 2 | Type of college | 0.2958 | 0.08752 | 43.25** |
| 3 | Group | 0.3014 | 0.09085 | 30.01** |

**significant at .01 level.

Out of five independent variables the variable 'gender' has entered first in step wise regression equation. With R2.08348. It is significant at.01 level. Its contribution is 8% to factor-Q1 as the increase in R2 due to this variable is significant it was retained in the equation F-value is 82.25.

The variable 'type of the college' was entered in the second step, since it has the highest partial correlation and consequently higher "F" value to enter 43.25552 which is significant at .01 levels the addition of thins variable has increased the R2 by 0.00404 that is it additionally accounted for .4% of the variance to factor-Q1. The combination of the two variables (R2 .08752) explains 8% of the variance to factor-Q1.

In the third step, 'group' was entered as that has the next highest "F" to enter 30.01056. this variable has additionally contributed about .00333.that is .3% of the variance to factorQ1 as is shown by the increase in R2.the combination of the three variables accounted for .9% of the variance to factor-Q1.

The other two variables have not entered in stepwise regression as there values were insignificant.

Hence the hypothesis that "there is no significant effect of demographical factors on personality factor- Q1" is not accepted.

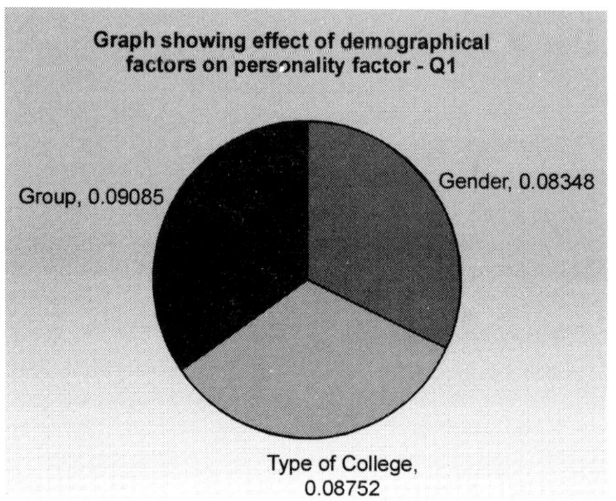


### Hypothesis-38

"There is no significant effect of demographical variables on personality factor-Q2".

### Factor–Q2

Five independent variables have not entered in stepwise regression as there values were insignificant.

Hence the hypothesis that "there is no significant effect of demographical factors on personality factor-Q2"gets accepted.

### Hypothesis-39

"There is no significant effect of demographical factors on personality factor-Q3".

Results pertaining to this hypothesis are presented in the table 5.25.

**Table 5.25. Showing Step-wise Regression Analysis for Personality Factor-Q3 and Demographical Factors**

| S. No. | Variable | R | R2 | F-value To enter |
|---|---|---|---|---|
| 1. | Type of college | 0.0933 | 0.00870 | 7.92** |
| 2. | Gender | 0.1246 | 0.01552 | 7.107** |

**significant at .01 level

Out of five independent variables 'type of the college' has entered first in step wise regression as it has highest zero order correlation with factor-Q3 in the regression equation. The R2 for type of the college is .00870. It is significant at .01 levels. And its contribution is .8%. As the increase in R2 due to this variable is significant it was retained in the equation F-value is 7.92.

The variable 'gender' was entered in the second step, since it has the highest partial correlation and consequently higher "F" to enter 7.107643 which is significant at .01 level. The additional of this variable has increased the R2 by .00682 that is it additionally accounted for .6% of the variance to factor-Q3. The combination of the two variables (R2.01552) explains 1% of the variance to factor-Q3.

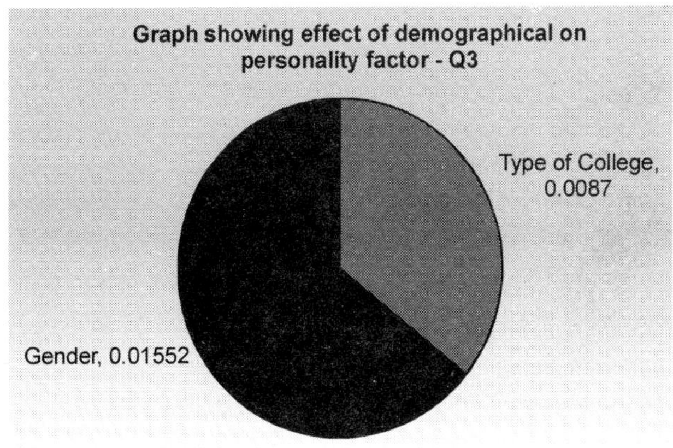

The other three variables have not entered in step wise regression as their values were insignificant.

Hence the hypothesis "that there is no significant effect of demographical factors on personality factorsQ3"gets rejected.

## Hypothesis-40

"There is no significant effect of demographical factors on personality factor-Q4."

Results pertaining to this hypothesis are presented in the table 5.26.

**Table 5.26. Showing Step-wise Regression of Personality Factor-Q4 and Demographical Factors**

| S. No. | Variable | R | R2 | F-value To enter |
|---|---|---|---|---|
| 1. | Group | 0.1540 | 0.02371 | 21.93** |
| 2. | Gender | 0.1776 | 0.03153 | 14.682** |

**significant at .01 level.

Out five independent variables the variable that has entered first in stepwise analysis is 'group' with high F-value 21.9341 and R2 is 0.02371which is significant at .01 levels. And its contribution is 2% for personality factor Q4.

The variable 'gender' was entered in the second step, since it has the highest partial correlation and consequently higher "F" to enter 14.68 which is significant at .01 Levels. The addition of this variable.

Has increased the R2 by .0782. That is, it additionally accounted for 7% of the variance to personality factor-Q4.the combination two variables (R20.03153) explains 3% of the variance to personality factor Q4.

The other three variables have not entered in the step wise regression as their values were not significant.

Hence the hypothesis that "there is no significant effect of demographical factors on personality factor-Q4"gets rejected.

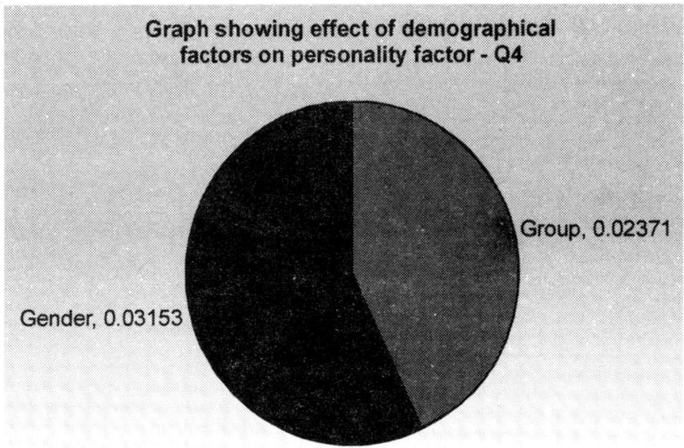


"There is no significant effect of demographical factors on 16 personality factors"

Results pertaining to this hypothesis are presented in the table.

## TOTAL 16-PERSONALITY FACTORS AND DEMOGRAPHICAL FACTORS

Five independent variables for 16-personality factors have not entered in step wise regression equation as there values were not significant.

Hence the hypothesis "there is no significant relation between demographical factors and 16-personality factors" gets accepted.

# SUMMARY, CONCLUSIONS

The present investigation was undertaken to find out the relationship between self-efficacy and intelligence, personality and occupational choice among intermediate students and to find out the effect of gender, nativity, parents educational qualifications, and type of the college, and group (subject) on the four selected variables.

The results have been presented in the previous chapter. This chapter presents the summary of the previous chapter in a nut shell.

## Summary Related to Chapter-I

In the first chapter importance of the research problem was discussed taking into consideration four variables self-efficacy, intelligence, personality, and occupational choice relating each other.

In the outset Career choice, career determinants, changing trends in career choice aims and nature of occupational information, common mistakes made in occupational selection, were discussed with various factors affecting it.

Secondly importance of self-efficacy beliefs in the life of the individual was discussed with Banduras social cognitive theory. Then various sources of self-efficacy beliefs were listed out along with efficacy activated process.

Then effects of self-efficacy beliefs and its importance in career choice were discussed.

Thirdly self-efficacy beliefs were related to personality traits and various types of personality types along with their occupational preferences based on Anne Roe's childhood determinants of vocational choice were discussed.

At the end importance of mental ability (intelligence) and occupational preferences, were discussed.

## Summary Related to Chapter-II

In the second chapter the reviews of research related to self-efficacy, intelligence, personality, and occupational choice of students and teachers were presented.

## Summary Related to Chapter-III

In the third chapter problem of the research has been stated, its significance was discussed, objectives were stated, hypotheses were formulated, and variables of the study were explained.

## Significance of the Problem

"There is only one success- to be able to spend your life in your own way." -Christopher Morley

In today's world, which is marked by competition, it is imperative to manage the stress and strain to keep pace with demands of the society, changing trends, and great expectations. Because only that individual who is successful in all aspects, is the survival of the fittest in this world Educational field is also not an exception, as globalisation posess a number of challenges.

Present educational system has failed to bring an all round development in the individual. It may be because of faulty examination oriented education, which compels the students to mug up the stereotype questions and answers and just present as it is in examinations without any thought and insight into the subject matter. It is laying more emphasis on the knowledge and information aspect. Our educational system has literally failed to develop life skills which are essential for future of the student. Lack of proper guidance at different stages left child confused. Overburdened curriculum, corporate educational system, great expectations of the teachers and parents is making the children more stress prone and leading to more psychological problems, insecurity, negative competitions, and developing suicidal tendencies among school and college students. Students due to the lack of proper guidance and awareness at intermediate level are opting for stereotype jobs or jobs of their peer choice and lamenting over their choice later which has resulted in job dissatisfaction, maladjustment and inability to cope up with arising needs.

Students success in life depends upon their intelligence bestowed through their heredity, the personality traits they have acquired through their environment (family, school, peer, neighbors, and physical environment) child rearing practices (discipline, instructions given ,guidance provided, facilities provided, physical and psychological need satisfaction),their personality traits, and personal experiences.

Real contentment in life could be achieved only by having faith in ones abilities, purposeful thought and reasoning, taking right decision at right time and optimistic attitude in life.

Present study is significant as it throws light on the self-efficacy believes in the intermediate students their personality traits, their intelligence and its influence on their occupational choice.

There is a growing body of evidence that human accomplishments and positive well-being require an optimistic sense of personal efficacy. This is because ordinary social realities are strewn with difficulties. They are full of impediments, adversities, setbacks, frustrations, and inequities. People must have a robust sense of personal efficacy to sustain the perseverant effort needed to succeed. In pursuits strewn with obstacles, realists either forsake them, abort their efforts prematurely when difficulties arise or become cynical about the prospects of effecting significant changes.

It is widely believed that misjudgment breeds personal problems. Certainly, gross miscalculation can get one into trouble. However, the functional value of accurate self-appraisal depends on the nature of the activity. Activities in which mistakes can produce costly or injurious consequences call for accurate self-appraisal of capabilities. It is a different matter where difficult accomplishments can produce substantial personal and social benefits and the costs involve one's time, and expendable resources. People with high sense of efficacy have the staying power to endure the obstacles and set backs that characterise difficult undertakings.

When people err in their self appraisal they tend to overestimate their capabilities. Their is a benefit rather than a cognitive failing to be eradicated. Self- efficacy beliefs always reflected only what people can do routinely they would rarely fail but they would not set aspirations beyond their immediate reach nor mount the extra effort needed to surpass their ordinary performances.

In sum, the successful, the venturesome, the sociable, the non-anxious, the non-depressed, the social reformers, and the innovators take an optimistic view of their personal capabilities to exercise influence over events that affect their lives. If not unrealistically exaggerated, such self beliefs foster positive well-being and human accomplishments.

Many of the challenges of life are group problems requiring collective effort to produce significant change. The strength of groups, organisations, and even nations lies partly in people's sense of collective efficacy that they can solve the problems they face and improve their lives through unified effort. People's beliefs in their collective efficacy influence what they choose to do as a group, how much effort they put into it, their endurance when collective efforts fail to produce quick results, and their likelihood of success.

The need of the hour is to boost up self-efficacy beliefs, build up self-confidence, and guide the students in right path by developing positive attitude in life, hard working nature, and good communicative skills.

Hence keeping in view the exiting problems of education, the researcher has selected the problem "self-efficacy in relation to intelligence, personality and occupational choice among intermediate students."

## Objective of the Study

The researcher has undertaken the research with the following objectives and to know the relationship between the following variables of the study.

1. To know the relationship between self efficacy and intelligence.
2. To know the relationship between self-efficacy and personality factors.
3. To know the significance difference of high or low self efficacy on 16-personality factors.
4. To know the significance difference of high or low intelligence on 16-personality factors.
5. To know the effect of gender on self-efficacy.
6. To know the effect of nativity on self-efficacy.
7. To know the effect of parents educational qualifications on self-efficacy.
8. To know the effect of type of the college on self-efficacy.
9. To know the effect of group (subject) on self-efficacy.
10. To know the effect of gender on intelligence.
11. To know the effect of nativity on intelligence.
12. To know the effect of parents educational qualifications on intelligence.
13. To know the effect of type of the college on intelligence.

14. To know the effect of group (subject) on intelligence.
15. To know the effect of demographical variables on personality factor-A (Aloof or warm and outgoing)
16. To know the effect of demographical variables on personality factor-B (Dull or Bright)
17. To know the effect of demographical variables on personality factor-C (Emotional or Mature)
18. To know the effect of demographical factors on personality factor-E (Submissive or dominant)
19. To the know the effect of demographical variables on personality factor-F (Glum, silent or enthusiastic)
20. To know the effect of demographical variables on personality factor-G (Casual or conscientious)
21. To know the effect of demographical variables on personality factor-H (Timid or adventurous)
22. To know the effect of demographical variables on personality factor- I (Tough or sensitive)
23. To know the effect of demographical variables on personality factor-L (Trustful or suspecting)
24. To know the effect of demographical variables on personality factor-M (Conventional or eccentric)
25. To know the effect of demographical variables on personality factor-N (Simple or sophisticated)
26. To know the effect of demographical variables on personality factor-O (Confident or Insecure)
27. To know the effect of demographical variables on personality factor-Q1 (Conservative or Experimenting)
28. To know the effect of demographical variables on personality factor-Q2 (Dependant or self sufficient)
29. To know the effect of demographical variables on personality factor-Q3 (Uncontrolled or self-controlled)
30. To know the effect of demographical variables on personality factor-Q4 (Stable or tense)

31. To know the effect of gender on first occupational choice.
32. To know the effect of nativity on first occupational choice.
33. To know the effect of parents educational qualifications on first occupational choice.
34. To know the effect of type of the college on first occupational choice.
35. To know the effect of group (subject) on first occupational choice.
36. To know the effect of gender on second occupational choice.
37. To know the effect of nativity on the second occupational choice.
38. To know the effect of parents educational qualifications on second occupational choice.
39. To know the effect of type of the college on second occupational choice.
40. To know the effect of group on second occupational choice.

## Hypotheses of the Study

1. There is no significant relationship between self-efficacy and intelligence
2. There is no significant relationship between self-efficacy and personality factors.
3. There is no significant difference of high or low self-efficacy on personality factors.
4. There is no significant difference of high or low intelligence on 16-personality factors.
5. There is no significant effect of gender on self-efficacy.
6. There is no significant effect of nativity on self-efficacy.
7. There is no significant effect of parent's educational qualifications on self-efficacy.

8. There is no significant effect of type of the college on self-efficacy.
9. There is no significant effect of group (subject) on self-efficacy.
10. There is no significant effect of gender on intelligence.
11. There is no significant effect of nativity on intelligence.
12. There is no significant effect of parent's educational qualifications on intelligence.
13. There is no significant effect of type of the college on intelligence.
14. There is no significant effect of group (subject) on intelligence.
15. There is no significant effect of demographical variables on personality factor-A (Aloof or warm and outgoing)
16. There is no significant effect of demographical variables on personality factor-B (Dull or bright)
17. There is no significant effect of demographical variables on personality factor-C (Emotional or mature)
18. There is no significant effect of demographical variables on personality factor-E (Submissive or dominant)
19. There is no significant effect of demographical variables on personality factor-F (Glum, silent or enthusiastic)
20. There is no significant effect of demographical variables on personality factor-G (Casual or conscientious)
21. There is no significant effect of demographical variables on personality factor-H (Timid or adventurous)
22. There is no significant effect of demographical variables on personality factor-I (Tough or Sensitive)

23. There is no significant effect of demographical variables on personality factor-L (Trustful or suspecting)
24. There is no significant effect of demographical variables on personality factor-M (Conventional or eccentric)
25. There is no significant effect of demographical variables on personality factor-N (simple or sophisticated)
26. There is no significant effect of demographical variables on personality factor- O (Confident or insecure)
27. There is no significant effect of demographical variables on personality factopr-Q1 (Conservative or experimenting)
28. There is no significant effect of demographical variables on personality factor-Q2 (Dependent or sufficient)
29. There is no significant effect of demographical variables on personality factor_Q3 (Uncontrolled or self-controlled)
30. There is no significant effect of demographical variables on personality factor-Q4 (Stable or tense)
31. There is no significant effect of gender on first occupational choice.
32. There is no significant effect of nativity on first occupational choice.
33. There is no significant effect of parent's educational qualifications on first occupational choice.
34. There is no significant effect of type of the college on first occupational choice.
35. There is no significant effect of group (subject) on first occupational choice.
36. There is no significant effect of gender of second occupational choice.

37. There is no significant effect of nativity on second occupational choice.
38. There is no significant effect of parent's educational choice on second occupational choice.
39. There is no significant effect of type of the college on second occupational choice.
40. There is no significant effect of group (subject) on second occupational choice.

## Variables of the Study

**(*a*) Self-efficacy :** It is the belief in one's capability to organise and execute the course of action required to manage prospective situations.

**(*b*) Intelligence :** It is the aggregate of global capacity of the individual to act purposefully, to think rationally and to deal effectively with his environment-Wechsler.

Intelligence is the ability to undertake activities that are characterised by (1) difficulty (2) complexity (3) abstraction (4) economy (5) adaptiveness to a goal (6) social, value (7) and the emergence of the originals, and to maintain such activities under conditions that demand a consideration of energy and resistance to emotional force-Stoddard.

Terman defining intelligence says "an individual is intelligent in proportion as he is able to carry on abstract thinking."

Intelligence, the dictionary says, is "The capacity to acquire and apply knowledge."

**(*c*) Personality :** All port says "Personality is the dynamic organisation within the individual of those psychophysical systems that determine his unique adjustment to his environment".

Warren's dictionary defines personality, "personality is the integrative organisation of all the cognitive, affective, con-native and physical characteristics of an individual as it manifests itself in focal distinction from others".

Mark Sherman says" personality is the characteristic pattern of behaviours, cognitions, and emotion which may be experienced by the individual and manifest to others".

Freedenberg "personality is a stable system of complex characteristics by which the life pattern of the individual may be identified".

**(*d*) Occupational Choice :** It is conscious choice of an occupation based on truthful analysis of ones own personality, his likes and dislikes his special aptitudes, and his handicaps to arouse his latent talents.

**Sex**: Girls and boys studying in Intermediate colleges

**Locality** or nativity here means Rural intermediate students of countryside. Urban intermediate students of city municipality.

**(*g*) Parent's educational qualification :** includes illiterates, ssc, and intermediate, graduation, and post graduation.

**(*h*) Type of the college :** here it means Government College, Aided College, Unaided College, and Minority College.

**(*i*) Group**: The students studying in intermediate colleges are divided into four groups. They are

Mathematics physics and chemistry (MPC)

Biological science physics and chemistry (BPC)

History economics and civics (HEC)

Commerce economics and civics (CEC)

## Methodology

In the fourth chapter design of the study, sample selected, tools used and data collecting procedure was discussed.

## Sample of the Study

Nine hundred intermediate students (both girls and boys) studying in different colleges at Kurnool District constituted the sample for the study. First the number of colleges in Kurnool District were listed. Through stratified random sampling in total sixteen colleges were selected of which four are Government Institutions, Four aided Institutions, four unaided Institutions and Four minority Institutions.

From each type 225 students of which 100 are boys and 125 are girls. Thus the total of 900 students of which 400 are boys and 500 are girls were selected which constitute the sample of present study.

## Tools Used

In this study the researcher has used the following tools.

1. **Self-efficacy scale** by Ralf Schwarzer & Matthias Jerusalem, 1993.
2. **Standard Progressive Matrices** (sets-A, B, C, D and E) by J.C.Raven 1958
3. **16-personality factor questionnaire** by Cattle (form-C) 1962.
4. **Occupational choice** (locally standardized)

## Data Collection Procedure

Through stratified random sampling technique researcher has selected intermediate colleges of Kurnool district. The researcher met the sample of 900 students in groups of 20 each. They were distributed self-efficacy questionnaire and RPM. After developing rapport they were explained the significance of the study and instructions were given accordingly.

In second session 16 personality factors and occupational choice list was given and data was collected from all the 900 students. The responses of the subject were scored accordingly and the obtained data was subjected to statistical analysis. Such as t-values MRI.

## Statistical Analysis

The researcher has collected the required data from the

sample and, scores were given to each questionnaire as per the scoring key, and correlations, frequency distribution, mean standard deviation, and t-values and f-values were computed for obtained data.

## Results and Discussions

In the sixth chapter results pertaining to various hypotheses were presented and discussed comprehensively, in the nutshell.

## Summary of Results and Discussions

1. There is significant relationship between self efficacy and intelligence.
2. There is no significant correlations between self efficacy and 16 Personality Factors.
3. There is no significant difference of High or low self efficacy on 16 Personality Factors.
4. There is no significant difference of High or low intelligence on 16 Personality Factors.
5. There is no significant effect of gender, nativity, Education Qualification of parents, type of the college and group on self efficacy in multiple regression analysis.
6. There is no significant effect of gender, nativity, and type of the college on Intelligence. But this is significant of group and placation education qualifications on intelligence of children in MRA.
7. There is no significant effect of gender, nativity, education qualifications of parents on first occupation choice of studies but there is significant effect of type of the college and group (subject) on first occupation choice in MRA.
8. There is no significant effect of gender, nativity, education of parents and type of the college as second occupation choice of students. But However group or

subject has effect as second occupational choice in MRA.

9. Step-wise regression analysis for personality factor – A and demographical factor depends that there is significant effect of group, type of the college and education qualification of parents on personality factor – A is being along as women out going where as other two factors i.e., nativity and gender do not have any significant effect an factor –A
10. There is significant effect of nativity on personality factor – B That is being dull or bright. But the other demographical factor such as gender, type of the college, group, parents education qualifications do not have any effect on personality factor –B.
11. There is significant effect of gender on personality factor –C that is being emotion or mater but other factor do not have any effect.
12. There is significant effect of parents education Qualifications and nativity on Personality Factors - E ie, being submissive or dominos other factors do not have any impact on Personality Factors - E
13. There is significant effect of gender and group on Personality Factors - F i.e, being glum, silent are being enthusiastic. The other three factor do not have any effect on Personality Factors-F
14. There is significant effect of type the college, gender, Parents education 'Q' on Personality Factors-G. i.e. being casual or can conscientious the other two factor have no significant effect.
15. There is no significant effect of gender, nativity, parents education 'Q', type of the college, group on Personality Factors-H i.e. being timid or adventurous.
16. There is no significant effect of gender nativity, parental education, type of the college & group on Personality Factors-I i.e. being tough or sensitive

17. There is no significant effect of gender, nativity, Parent's education group & type of the college on Personality Factors-L i.e. being trustful or suspects
18. There is significant effect of gender on Personality factor – M i.e. but conventional or eccentric and the other factors such as nativity, group, parent's education and type of the college do not have significant effect on personality factor – M.
19 There is significant effect of gender on Personality factor – N i.e. being simple or sophistication. The other demographical factor such as nativity, group, type of the college, parent's education have no significant effect on Personality factor – N.
20. There is no significant effect of nativity, gender, group, type of the college, and parent's education on the factor – 'O' i.e. being confident or being insecure.
21. There is significant effect of gender, type of the college and group on Personality factor – Q1 i.e. being conservative or experimented. The other two factors such as nativity and parent education have no signification effect.
22. There is no significant effect of gender halvah's type of the college, group & parent's education on Personality factor – Q2 i.e. being dependent or self suffices.
23. There is significant effect of type of the college, and gender on Personality factor – Q3 i.e. being uncontrolled or self-controlled. The other factor nativity, group education have no significant effect.
24. There is significant effect of group gender on Personality factor – Q4 i.e. being stable or tense. The other three factor nativity, type of the college and education of parents have no significant effect on Personality factor – Q4.

25. There is no significant effect of gender, nativity group, parents education and type of the college on 16 personality factors.

## Conclusion

This research was intended to find out the relation, significance difference and effect of selected variables self efficacy, intelligence and 16-personality factors and occupational choice for the same purpose, t-value, F-values were computed.

In the first stage the research investigation proved that there is positive corelation between self-efficacy and intelligence. That means higher the self efficacy higher the intelligence is. Hence it is essential to boost up self efficacy and enhance mental ability of students at various levels.

Secondly there is no significant corelation found between self efficacy and 16-personality factors and also no significance difference of high or low self efficacy on 16 personality factors in research investigation.

In third step researcher tried to find out if there is any significant difference of high or low intelligence as 16-Personalty factor.

Results depicted that there is no significant difference or effect of high or low intelligence on 16-Personality factor. It means personality traits are not effected by intelligence.

Then researcher investigated to find out the effect of various selected demographical factors on gender, nativity, parents educational qualifications, group and type of the college on self efficacy, intelligence personality and occupation choice.

No significant effect of Demographical factors on self efficacy was found However, intelligence is effected by educational qualification of parents, and the group they have opted for.

Results reveal that occupational choice of students is effected or influenced by the group or the subject at (10+2) level, apart from this type of college whether it is Government, aided, unaided or minority institution has shown impact an occupational preference, may be because of the awareness exposure, guidance from peer group, and tutors.

Stepwise regression analysis for various personality factors and demographical factors was made to find out how personality traits get effected by gender, nativity, parents education, type of the college and group.

Whether the students are aloof or out going depend on parents education, subject or group and type of the college. Parent's sociability, interest of the student in subject effect his traits.

Almost all the demographical factors have impact on 16-Personality factor however, it was found out that students of urban background whose parents are highly qualified and can encourage children and provide proper facility for them, join in good colleges with subject of their interest have shown better personality traits than those who are deprived of it.

Hence research results emphasize the role of parents and teacher in modifying the behaviour and personality traits of children accordingly.

# EDUCATIONAL IMPLICATIONS, SUGGESTIONS FOR FUTURE STUDY

## Introduction

In the previous chapter results pertaining to various hypotheses were presented along with discussions. This chapter presents educational implications of the study based on results of statistical analysis.

The ultimate aim of educational system is to make the child self-dependent not only to earn bread and butter for his life, but also to develop independent thought to judge between good and bad, best and worst. And to take right decision at right time by analyzing the situation in which the individual is placed.

Primarily it is the responsibility of the parents and teachers to work together for the growth and development of the children. Parents brought up, rearing practices, the attitude they have the environment they provide at home, their sociability the encouragement they provide, and their educational qualifications are very essential factors which reflects the behaviour of the child.

This is possible only when the teacher, apart from teaching has to shoulder some additional responsibilities of observing the children, their personality traits, their mental abilities in the class room and guide them in proper way.

Hence based up on the statistical analysis, discussions and research results the following educational implications were suggested.

## Educational Implications

- In modern competitive world children fail to achieve their goal with little difference, and then they become pessimistic. It is essential to enhance their self-efficacy beliefs by developing self-confidence, belief in oneself, or a sense of personal power.
- Developing emotionally enhanced "faith" or enthusiasm or zeal about ones ability to change one self or a problem situation..
- High feeling of confidence might be generated by watching a person who is in same situation, and mastered the situation.
- Presenting examples of those who have successfully coped with serious problems, describing their techniques, setbacks, traumas, and other emotionally meaningful or moving experiences.
- Providing actual uplifting experiences to know that students have more control over themselves.
- Making the students to realise the fact that their success is the results of their high ability and their failure is results of lack of effort.
- Children should be made to learn to accept failure and feel confident in ones self-help-ability. To feel less stress, and take more risks and try harder and longer to make the changes.
- A depressed person remembers previous failures while confident people remember past successes which influence self-efficacy estimates. A good mood and a healthy comfortable body generate positive expectations.
- Importance of guidance cells in educational institutions (10 and 10+2) to enlighten the students about various professions, their nature of jobs, future prospects, income etc.

- Compulsory Recruitment of counsellors in educational institutions to council the students in educational and real life.
- Conduction of awareness programmes in relation to various jobs in schools and colleges. At 10 and 10+2 stage.
- Taking the students to job melas.
- Assessing the abilities, and skills of students using psychological tests. and boosting positive self-efficacy beliefs.
- Providing educational and vocational guidance in the educational institutions.
- Helping the students to take up professions according to their abilities and interests.
- Making the students aware of different types of organisations which provide financial help to the students to get higher education.
- Hence both girls and boys must be educated irrespective of gender bias.
- Parents must encourage the girl child to study and send their children to school.
- Parents should not hesitate to invest money on the education of girl child.
- Irrespective of rural or urban background students must be encouraged to study by providing better facilities.
- Rural student's self-efficacy beliefs must be boosted up as they have poor learning environment.
- Equal encouragement must be given to rural students along with urban students.

It was rightly said that "if a women gets educated whole family gets educated where as if a man gets educated he alone is educated."

- Proper awareness must be provided to the parents to improve their educational qualifications.

- Educating parents related to the course of their children, guiding them to help the child.
- Parents must provide better environment, facilities, and enlighten their children related to various aspects of life.
- Students must be encouraged to choose the professional courses according the societal needs.
- There is a need to change the curriculum to make it more innovative, and creative.
- Stereotyped courses must be removed.
- Mostly middle class people prefer private, aided and corporate colleges; hence it is the need of the hour to establish English medium government colleges accessible to the poor.
- Innovative courses must be introduced in government colleges.
- At 10+2 level the group the students opt for is turning point for their life. Hence wise choice must be made based on their abilities and interest.
- Selection of the college is also an important aspect to remember. Hence right type of college with good teaching staff, which imparts qualitative education, must be selected.

It was observed that the students do not have knowledge of their abilities.

Hence the students with low self-efficacy have chosen high professions like doctor, engineer architect, astronomer, collector politician, judge etc.

Where as the students with high self-efficacy have chosen diversified professions which are challenging. Hence one must remember that one should not overestimate ones abilities and be realistic.

## Suggestions for Future Study

It was in 1986 Bandura has introduced the concept of self-efficacy.

Since then many foreign researchers tried to find out the effect of self-efficacy beliefs on scholastic achievement, motivation, managerial effectiveness, and teachers self-efficacy. Very few studies were conducted on self-efficacy in India as this is a latest and novel concept.

Future study can be conducted on the following areas to bring out more facts into light.

## Study Areas of School Children

- Self-efficacy of school going children in relation to various school subjects.
- Self-efficacy and coping strategies of examination stress.
- Self-efficacy and judging, reasoning ability.
- Self-efficacy and problem solving ability.
- Self-efficacy and scholastic achievement, motivation, self-satisfaction.
- Self-efficacy, personality traits and intelligence
- Self-efficacy and group (subject) preferences at 10+ levels.
- Self-efficacy of exceptional children like, physically handicapped, deaf, dumb, crippled, blind, and children with low mental abilities.
- Self-efficacy of highly intelligent and gifted children.
- Self-efficacy beliefs of scheduled caste, and scheduled tribes children residing in hostels in relation to material facilities and achievement motivation.
- Comparative study on self-efficacy of forward caste and backward caste children in relation to motivation and achievement.
- Self-efficacy of students studying in Navodaya schools in comparison to normal schools.

**Study Areas of Teachers**

- Primary schools teachers' self-efficacy and problem solving ability.
- High school teachers self-efficacy and performance.
- Self-efficacy and job satisfaction of .school teachers, DIET teachers, B.Ed lecturers.
- Self-efficacy beliefs and scientific attitude among science and mathematics teachers.
- Self-efficacy beliefs and administrative effectiveness of Head masters, or principals.
- Self-efficacy beliefs of various professionals in relation to their professions.
- Self-efficacy beliefs of parents and its impact on the self-efficacy of their children.

# BIBLIOGRAPHY


| S. No. | Author | Year | Title |
|---|---|---|---|
| 1. | D.A.Adeyemo & Bolaogumyemi | 1985 | "Emotional intelligence and self efficacy as a predictor of occupational stress on academic staff in Nigerian University". |
| 2. | Appeal baum & Tuma | 1977 | Validity of WISE, WISE-R for two socio-economic groups. |
| 3. | Anderson & Brewer | 1965 | Influence of classroom personality on children's behaviour. |
| 4. | Ajay Rao | 1978 | Intelligence tests. |
| 5. | Bandura | 1986 | "Self-efficacy beliefs, motivation, and achievement in writing". |
| 6. | Bandura | 1989 | Self regulation of motivation and action through standards and goal system. |
| 7. | Bandura | 1997 | Self efficacy the exercise of control. |
| 8. | Bandara | 1998 | Developing efficacy beliefs in the classroom. |
| 9. | Berry | 1987 | Perceived self efficacy in cognitive development and functioning. |
| 10. | Brophy | 1998 | Developing efficacy beliefs in the classroom. |
| 11. | Brown & Inouye | 1978 | Intervention strategies to increase self efficacy and self-regulation. |

| | | | |
|---|---|---|---|
| 12. | Bouffard-Bouchard | 1990 | Self efficacy in college students. |
| 13. | Belmont & Marolla | 1973 | Socio economic status and birth order effects. |
| 14. | Bechar | 1987 | Effect of Managerial styles. |
| 15. | Bowin | 1987 | Personality traits of successful managers. |
| 16. | Bush | 1988 | Personality profiles of Marketing Vs. research and developmental managers. |
| 17. | Borg | 1957 | Personality and internal measures related to criteria of instructor effectiveness. |
| 18. | Barbara, Sherman, Robert & Black Burn | 1975 | Personal characters & teacher effectiveness of college faculty. |
| 19. | Bhagoli | 1982 | Personality Characters Associated with Teaching Effectiveness through research Technique. |
| 20. | Barials | 1966 | Effect of social class on scholastic achievement. |
| 21. | Batlies | 1979 | Personality attributes of supervisor. |
| 22. | Boemister and Bartlett | 1962 | The freedom from distractibility factor and examination of its adaptive behaviour correlates. |
| 23. | Bali | 1981 | Personality factors of highly creative person in different fields. |
| 24. | Chapmen & Tunmer | 1995 | Reading Performance of beginning reader during their first year of schooling. |
| 25. | Collins | 1982 | Mathematics ability and self-efficacy. |
| 26. | G.V.Caprara | 1999 | Role of Perceived cognitive and environmental barriers on self-efficacy shapes of |

| | | | |
|---|---|---|---|
| | | | children's aspiration and career Trajectories. |
| 27. | Covin | 1977 | Relationships between peabody WISE-R, IQs of candidates for special education. |
| 28. | Cohen | 1959 | Analysis of factorial structure of the WISC. |
| 29. | Chatterji, Mukherji, Benerji | 1972 | Effect of Demographical variables on Scholastic achievement of VI and VII students. |
| 30. | Crunbach | 1960 | Usefulness of vocational inter. Measurers on managerial effectiveness. |
| 31. | Chakravarthi | 1984 | Assessment of personality variables related to management role. |
| 32. | Charter and waples | 1966 | Personality traits of teachers and classroom effcctivoness. |
| 33. | Chhaya | 1974 | Comparison of effective and ineffective teacher in respect to personality adjustment teaching attitude and emotional stability. |
| 34. | Chouhan | 1985 | Principles and Techniques of guidance. |
| 35. | Chan D.W. | 2003 | Multiple intelligence and perceived self-efficacy among Chinese secondary teachers. |
| 36. | Don. E. Bradley & James A.Robert | 1987 | Self employment and Job satisfaction in relation to role of self-efficacy and seniority. |
| 37. | Davis | 1978 | IQ of Deprived children. |
| 38. | Derr | 1987 | Study on managerial skills. |
| 39. | Erikson | 1959, 1980 | The social Psychology of self efficacy. |

| | | | |
|---|---|---|---|
| 40. | Eva Sehmitt Rodermund | 1991 | Adults career choice in East and West. |
| 41. | Ernest.Hilgard & Atkinson Rital Atkinson | 1980 | Introduction to psychology. |
| 42. | Edutracks-September | 2005 | Intelligence and academic Achievement. |
| 43. | Edutracks-January | 2006 | Self concept among school children. |
| 44. | Edutracks-August | 2006 | Emotional intelligence and copied resources as street. |
| 45. | Edutracks- May | 2006 | Self concept. |
| 46. | Edutracks-April | 2007 | Self-directed Learning. |
| 47. | Graham & Weiner | 1995 | Increasing memory and self-efficacy. |
| 48. | Giselle | 1966 | Executive Effectiveness and intelligence. |
| 49. | Gable | 1990 | Managerial achievement on Machiavellianism and internality and externality. |
| 50. | Getzel and Jackson | 1963 | Personality Traits of good teachers. |
| 51. | Guyton J John William | 1988 | Comparison on personality Traits of secondary school Teachers in Mississippi public school. |
| 52. | Goyal | 1974 | Personality correlation of secondary school teachers. |
| 53. | Gupta | 1975 | Teacher effectiveness through personality traits. |
| 54. | Grewal | 1976 | Teacher effectiveness and personality traits |
| 55. | Gupta | 1977 | Personality characterstic, adjustment level, academic achievement and personal attitude of successful teacher. |

| | | | |
|---|---|---|---|
| 56. | Gupta | 1981 | Comparative study of male and female teachers in the inventory as values, personality needs and moral judgement. |
| 57. | Hackett and Betz | 1989 | Career self-efficacy development and students with learning difficulties. |
| 58. | Harter | 1982 | Comparison between self concept and self efficacy academic. |
| 59. | Harter | 1990 | Comparison between self concept and self efficacy in academics. |
| 60. | Hanson and cox | 1987 | Developing self efficacy beliefs in the classroom. |
| 61. | Hung, Traci | 1990 | Influence of internet self efficacy and self-efficacy task on locating credible health related information online. |
| 62. | Hatch and cavin | 1977 | Comparative study of three groups in WISC. |
| 63. | Hagen and Kaufman | 1975 | Study of WISC-R factor in retarded and normal children. |
| 64. | Having Hurst & Moorefield | 1967 | Differences in IQS of disadvantaged and non-disadvantaged. |
| 65. | Horton and Crump | 1962 | Educational level of parents and IQ of their children. |
| 66. | Hammond and cox | 1967 | Importance of social class, mental ability and interpersonal competence as education achievement. |
| 67. | Harts fields, Michael Kirk | 2003 | Internal dynamics of transformation leadership effects of spirituality, emotional intelligence and self-efficacy. |

| | | | |
|---|---|---|---|
| 68. | Inderriedn | 1984 | Personality characteristics of work group managers and work group dimensions. |
| 69. | Jensen | 1969 | Effect of socio-economic state of middle and upper class intelligence. |
| 70. | Jorgensen | 1966 | Personality Traits of executive managers. |
| 71. | Jodd.J.Maurer | 2005 | Career relevant learning and development work age, beliefs about self efficacy. |
| 72. | Kaufman | 1975 | Factor analysis of WISC-R at age 6 to 16 years. |
| 73. | Kang, Jeonghee | 1998 | Memory self efficacy and memory performance. |
| 74. | Kellick and Leibouwitz | 1998 | Community based learning in marketing factors associated with it. |
| 75. | Kristine Haertl | 2002 | Mental illness in daily occupations. |
| 76. | Knife and Stroud | 1959 | Effect of intelligence on self efficacy. |
| 77. | Kaul | 1972 | Factorial study on personality variables of popular teachers in secondary schools. |
| 78. | Kum kum Tondon | 1980 | Career options after 10+2 science and technology. |
| 79. | Lent, Brown, Hackett | 1999 | Effect of family environment on personality and self efficacy on career decision of college students. |
| 80. | Lent | 1993 | Self efficacy judgements and learning out comes. |
| 81. | Lent and Hackett | 1987 | Decision making and self efficacy. |
| 82. | Lent, Brown and | 1984 | Self efficacy of college |
| | Larkin | 1986 | Students. |

| | | | |
|---|---|---|---|
| 83. | Levine | 1971 | Intelligence, Personality characters and motivation of in service and pre service Teachers. |
| 84. | Lokesh Kaul | 1975 | Attitude of school teachers towards teaching. |
| 85. | Lachman. M. EJelalian. E | 2006 | Self efficacy and attributions for intellectual performance in young and elderly adults. |
| 86. | Marsh | 1992 | Academic domain specific concept. |
| 87. | Marsh | 1991 | Effect of achievement and self concept and self efficacy. |
| 88. | Meece, Wigfield, Eccles | 1990 | Self efficacy beliefs in academic settings. |
| 89. | Meece | 1990 | Goal and self evaluation influences during children's cognitive development. |
| 90. | Mone, Backer and Jeffries | 1995 | Academic self efficacy as predity of college out comes |
| 91. | Metfessel | 1965 | Study of IQ of lower class children. |
| 92. | Mathur and Hundal | 1972 | Relationship between intelligence and socio-economic background. |
| 93. | Morris and Clarisio | 1977 | A study on High risk disadvantaged preschool children. |
| 94. | Moss | 1972 | A study on managerial success and related variables |
| 95. | Mohan | 1985 | Managerial effectiveness in relation to occupational goal values. |
| 96. | Mc.call, Appeal baum and Hogarthy | 1973 | Gap between children and intellectual levels. |
| 97. | Mc. Cleland | 1958 | Relationship between intelligence and achievement |

| | | | |
|---|---|---|---|
| 98. | Mathur | 1987 | Managerial effectiveness and leadership styles. |
| 99. | Mishra | 1979 | Personality traits of fluent teachers. |
| 100. | Nancy. E. Betz | 2000 | Decision making self efficacy |
| 101. | Nash, Guiun and Gattier | 1965<br>1966 | Personality and interest measures in managerial effectiveness. |
| 102. | Nicholson | 1977 | Study on correlation between WISC-R and quick tests. |
| 103. | Norman L. Munn and Dodge Fernandez Peter | 1990 | Introduction to psychology. |
| 104. | Oke chuku | 1994 | Retionship between six managerial charactertics and managerial effectiveness. |
| 105. | Pajer and Miller | 1994 | Item specific maths self efficacy. |
| 106. | Pintrich and Garcia | 1991 | Learning and individual differences |
| 107. | Pintrich and Degroot | 1990 | A model of meta cognition in achievement goal orientation learning. |
| 108. | Prakash | 1986 | Relationship between personal values of employees organisational outcome in banking organisation. |
| 109. | Paul | 1981 | Effect of personality on managerial effectiveness. |
| 110. | Pat Naik & Panda | 1982 | Personality and attitude patterns of good and poor teacher in secondary schools. |
| 111. | Peters and Williams | 1985 | Teachers intellectual disposition and students performance. |

| | | | |
|---|---|---|---|
| 112. | Phillips Wilson | 1984 | Job seeking self-efficacy for people with physical disability preliminary development and psychometric testing. |
| 113. | Reyes | 1984 | Role of self efficacy and self concept beliefs in mathematics. |
| 114. | Relich | 1983 | Maths self concept and maths achievement. |
| 115. | Rymarz | 1985 | Relationship between personality traits and levels of execution of professional tasks |
| 116. | Record | 1970 | IQ of single, Twins and triplets. |
| 117. | Radha Krishna | 1992 | Personality characteristic of high, low and moderate managerial effective groups. |
| 118. | Ryans | 1960 | Teachers attitudes and behaviour. |
| 119. | Robinson & Mc. Chael | 1987 | Personality traits of American Secondary Teacher and administrators. |
| 120. | Ramachandra Reddy | 1982 | Social Extroversion introversion in high school science teachers. |
| 121. | Ram Mishra | 1984 | Relationship between professional attitude and personality adjustment. |
| 122. | R.C. Sharma | 1986 | Advanced educational statistics. |
| 123. | Susan D. Phillipos and Anne R. Inhofe | 2007 | Women and career development. |
| 124. | Schunk | 1981 | Study on persuasions and verbal judgements. |
| 125. | Schunk | 1986 | Role of particularised self efficacy beliefs in various academic context. |

| | | | |
|---|---|---|---|
| 126. | Shell, Colvin and Brunung | 1989 | Measuring self efficacy multi trait, multi method comparisons. |
| 127. | Skaalvik and Rankin | 1996 | Comparison between self concept and self efficacy in Academic. |
| 128. | Schunk and Rice | 1993 | Perceived self efficacy. |
| 129. | Shell, Murphy & Burning | 1989 | Self efficacy reasoning ability and achievement in college Biology. |
| 130. | Smith | 1985 | Study on personality characteristics for personal selection. |
| 131. | Silverstein | 1964 | Analysis of WISC, WAIS, and WPPSI. |
| 132. | Silverstein | 1980 | Cluster analysis of WISC |
| 133. | Shuey | 1970 | IQs of Nigro children and Whites. |
| 134. | Sass, Kin, Marshall | 1987 | Difference between effective leader and management. |
| 135. | Singh and Satvir | 1989 | Variables effecting managerial success. |
| 136. | Savage | 1962 | Personality traits, academic performance and interpersonal skills. |
| 137. | Saxena | 1969 | Attitude and personality of teachers. |
| 138. | Srivastava | 1974 | Impact of professional experience on modification of personality traits. |
| 139. | Singh | 1974 | Personality profile of married and unmarried high school female teachers. |
| 140. | Sharma | 1975 | Relationship between personality factors and teaching effectiveness. |
| 141. | Singh | 1978 | Relation between teachers personality in teaching and impact on students behaviour. |

| | | | |
|---|---|---|---|
| 142. | Singh | 1978 | Leadership behaviour of the heads of secondary schools in Haryana. |
| 143. | Sharma | 1979 | Verbal class room behaviour of high school teachers |
| 144. | Sunder Raja, Sakthival and Ponnalagappan | 1988 | Attitude of men and women Bed teacher trainees. |
| 145. | Tracia Prodanuik and Ronal C. Plotnikoff | 2006 | Influence of self efficacy out comes expectation on the relationship between perceived environment and physical actives at work place. |
| 146. | Tarachand | 1986 | Educational psychology. |
| 147. | Thakur | 1980 | Personality characteristics of teachers showing direct and verbal behaviour. |
| 148. | Tripathi | 1972 | Personality profile of working teachers and teacher trainees |
| 149. | Valley, Hayashı, Holmer and Giacobbi | 1998 | Sport confidence |
| 150. | Verma and Sushila Devi | 1987 | Personality traits and job satisfaction of secondary school teachers. |
| 151. | Wender, Pedersen and Waldrop | 1967 | Social dependency and abstract cognitive style at 2 years of age. |
| 152. | Wayne and Blankenship | 1972 | Ideological orientation and personality characteristic of Teachers acceptance and rejection. |
| 153. | J.S.Walia | 1980 | Educational psychology. |
| 154. | Yvette Aqui | 1994 | Cognitive and motivational characteristics of adolescent gifted in mathmatics |
| 155. | Yergoror | 1990 | Personality Traits conductive for successful performance. |

| | | | |
|---|---|---|---|
| 156. | Zeidin and pajares | 1997 | Self efficacy beliefs of women in maths. |
| 157. | Zimmerman | 1991<br>1992 | The impact of reading self efficacy and the regulation. |
| 158. | Zimmerman | 1989,<br>1990,<br>1997 | The relationship to e-leaner self regulatory efficacy. |
| 159. | Zimmerman and Bandura | 1994 | Impact of self regulatory influence on writing course attainment. |
| 160. | Zimmerman and Ringle | 1981 | Self regulatory in academic learning and achievement. |
| 161. | Zimmerman, Martinez and pons | 1990 | Comparison between self concept and self efficacy in academics. |

## P



## Q



## R

❑❑❑